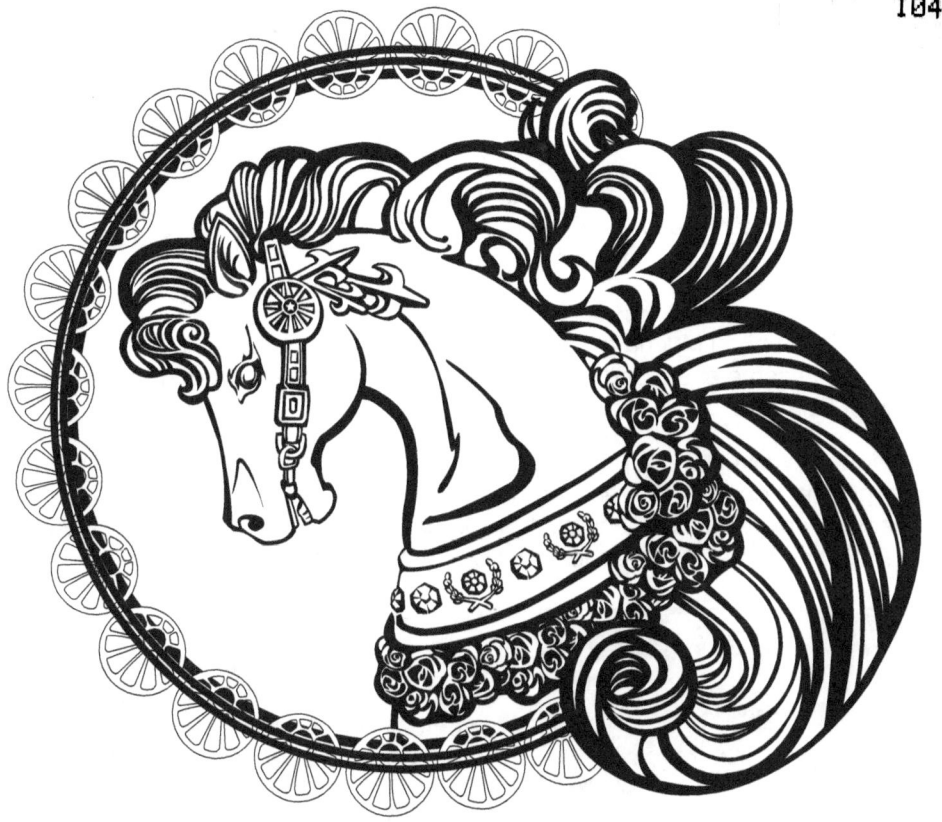

ART ESCAPES™
FINE ART COLORING BOOKS

DELUXE EDITION

Fine Art Coloring Book / Art History

Jennifer Kozlansky

Published 2015 by Kolzansky.com

*Special thanks to my dearest husband Scott
and my wonderful parents.*

FUNDRAISING AND CHARITY
Art Escapes™ Fine Art Coloring Books are perfect for fundraising and charity efforts.
Reach out on kozlansky.com/contact-us with your ideas.

Alphonse

Alphonse Maria Mucha is a Czech artist, known for inventing the Art Nouveau Movement.

Mucha loved to draw since childhood. As a young man, he painted theatrical scenery and also found work in decorative and portrait painting.

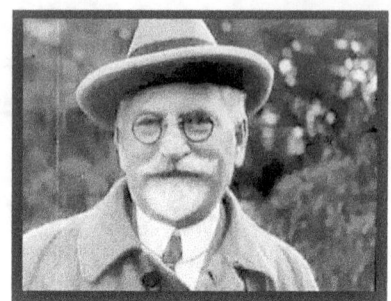

Alphonse Mucha 1860 - 1939

Count Karl Khuen hired Mucha to decorate Hrušovany Emmahof Castle with murals. Good ol' Karl became a fan, and sponsored Mucha's formal training at the Munich Academy of Fine Arts.

In 1894, Mucha walked into a print shop in Paris and learned there was an urgent need for a lithographed poster of Sarah Bernhardt. He offered to do the work and completed the project in two weeks. On January 1, 1895 the advertisement for the play was posted all over Paris and the artist received as much attention as the play!

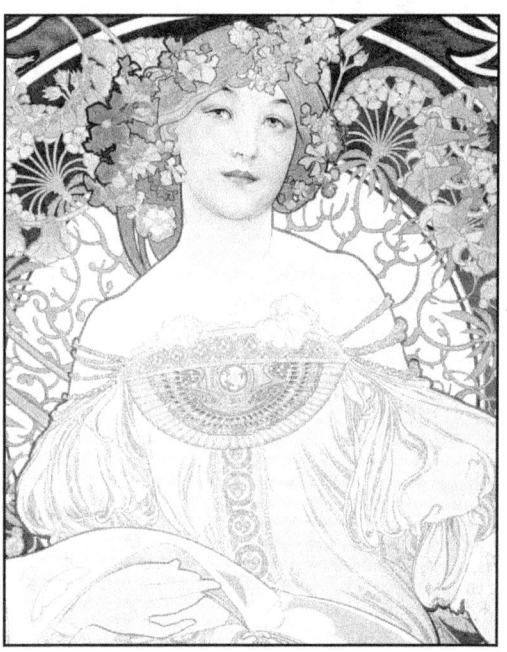

***F. Champenois* is a masterpiece created as an advertisment for Mucha's primary printer and lithographer.**

ART NOUVEAU

Art Nouveau, French for "new art", was originally called *Style Mucha*. This movement eventually influenced architecture, graphic arts, interior design and decorative arts.

In Mucha's work, we can see how the Art Nouveau style celebrates organic shapes. Sweeping, curved lines seem to dance off each other against lush patterns of flora.

He varied the thickness and darkness of his line to draw your attention to a particular area. He then distributed these areas carefully throughout the painting so the viewer's eye is moved through the work.

MUCHA'S FINE ART

The Slav Epic was considered by Mucha to be his fine art masterpiece. It is a series of twenty paintings, up to eight meters across, depicting the history of the Czech and Slavic people. He completed the work in 1928. It can be seen today at the National Gallery's Veletržní Palace.

NAZIS ARE MEAN

The 1930's saw a change in politics. Mucha's artwork, particularly the work focusing on Slav nationalism, fell out of favor. The local press declared his works reactionary and, when German troops entered Czechoslovakia in the spring of 1939, the aging artist was one of the first to be arrested and interrogated by the Gestapo. This harsh treatment was too much for Mucha, and he developed pneumonia. Despite his release, his health declined and he died on July 14,1939 of a lung infection.

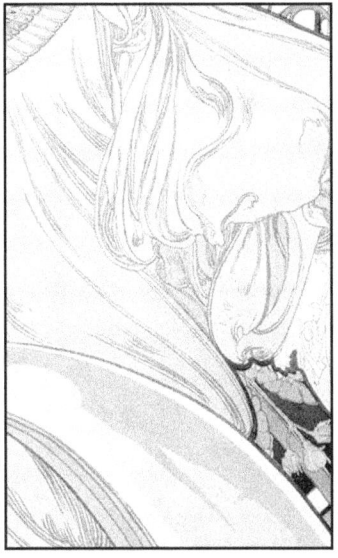

HOW ARTISTS CAN LEARN FROM MUCHA

Mucha was clearly a genius, especially when it came to line quality. So when you sketch on your own, always pay attention to your lines. Note how Mucha often groups multiple lines in certain areas, then reduces the number of lines, the weight of the line, or both, in other areas.

This gives the object visual weight, without the use of shading. It also results in more visual interest. If the line is the same weight throughout, it flattens the piece.

Draw from artists like Mucha and, most importantly, draw from life. Play around with line weight as you sketch your cat, a vase of flowers, anything and everything in real life.

Have a sketch you want to share? Looking for professional feedback on your work and more tips? Sign up for free on Kozlansky.com.

Jennifer

Jennifer has a BFA in Illustration from Ringling College of Art, Sarasota Florida. Always one to champion other's talent in any form, she genuinely adores art history.

She took postgraduate art history classes and interned at LCD Design in Florence Italy. When guiding her parents through art galleries, tourist groups gathered around as she gushed about the glorious artwork.

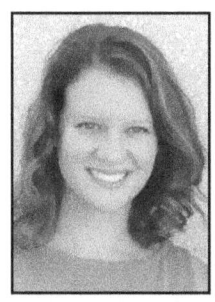

Jennifer Kozlansky

Despite it being one of the coldest recorded years in Italy, romance was still in the air. Jennifer fell in love... with the process of creating artwork with the Bézier curve.

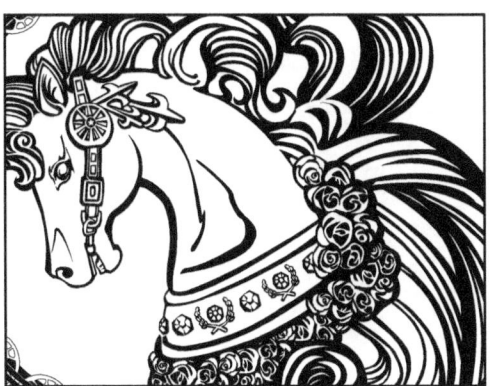

***The Rose Horse* was developed from one of Jennifer's sketchbooks.**

She met the Bézier curve on a tiny flickering Macintosh screen in the heart of Tuscany. Adobe's mid 90's *Birth of Venus* icon matched Botticelli's original *Birth of Venus* painting hanging in the Uffizi Museum down the street.

Still together today, Jennifer tries her best to keep things pretty. The artwork in this book was individually crafted with the Bézier curve. No automated process was used.

Jennifer lives with her husband in Pennsylvania, where she enjoys watching wildlife, volunteering and spending time with her family.

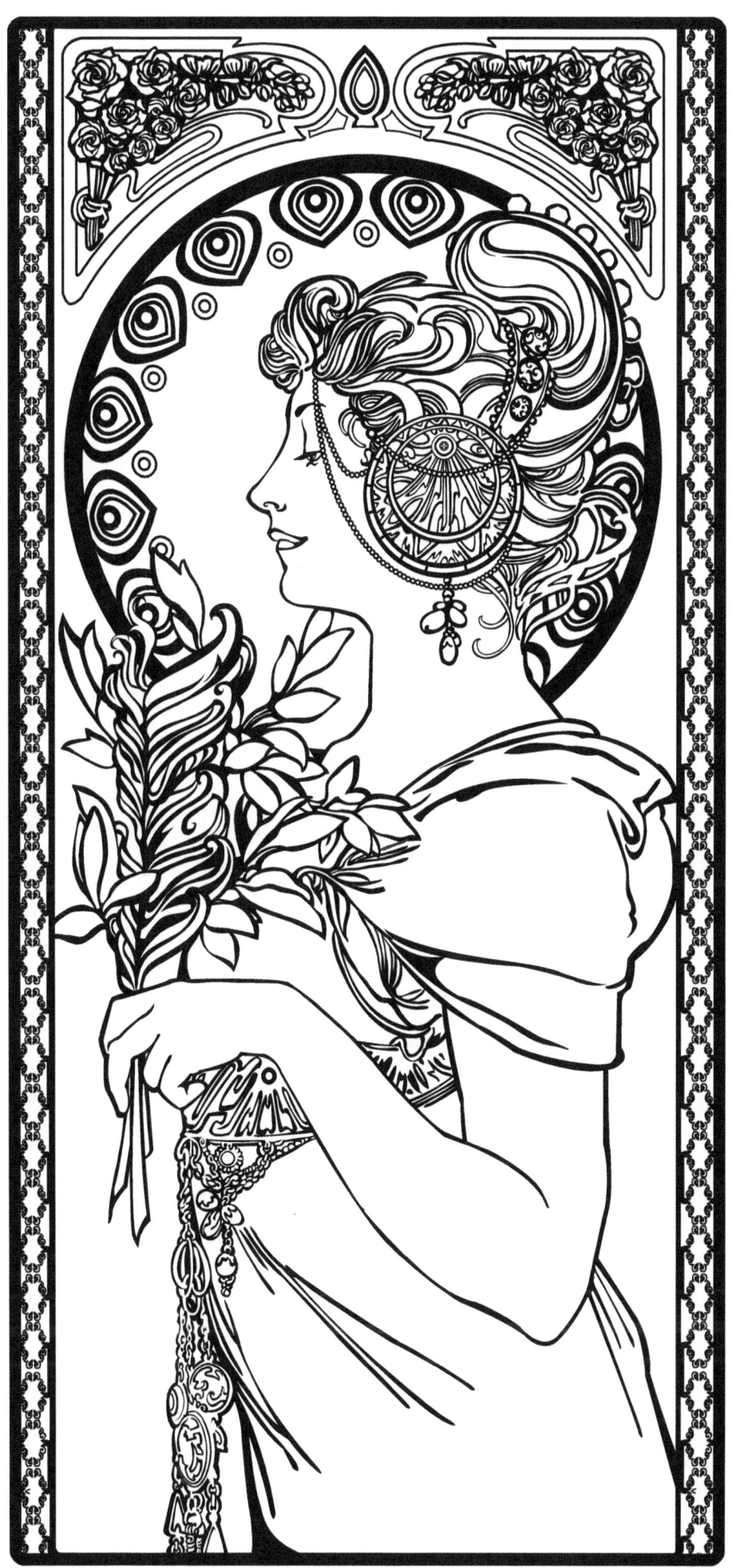

La Plume, 1899 Alphonse Mucha

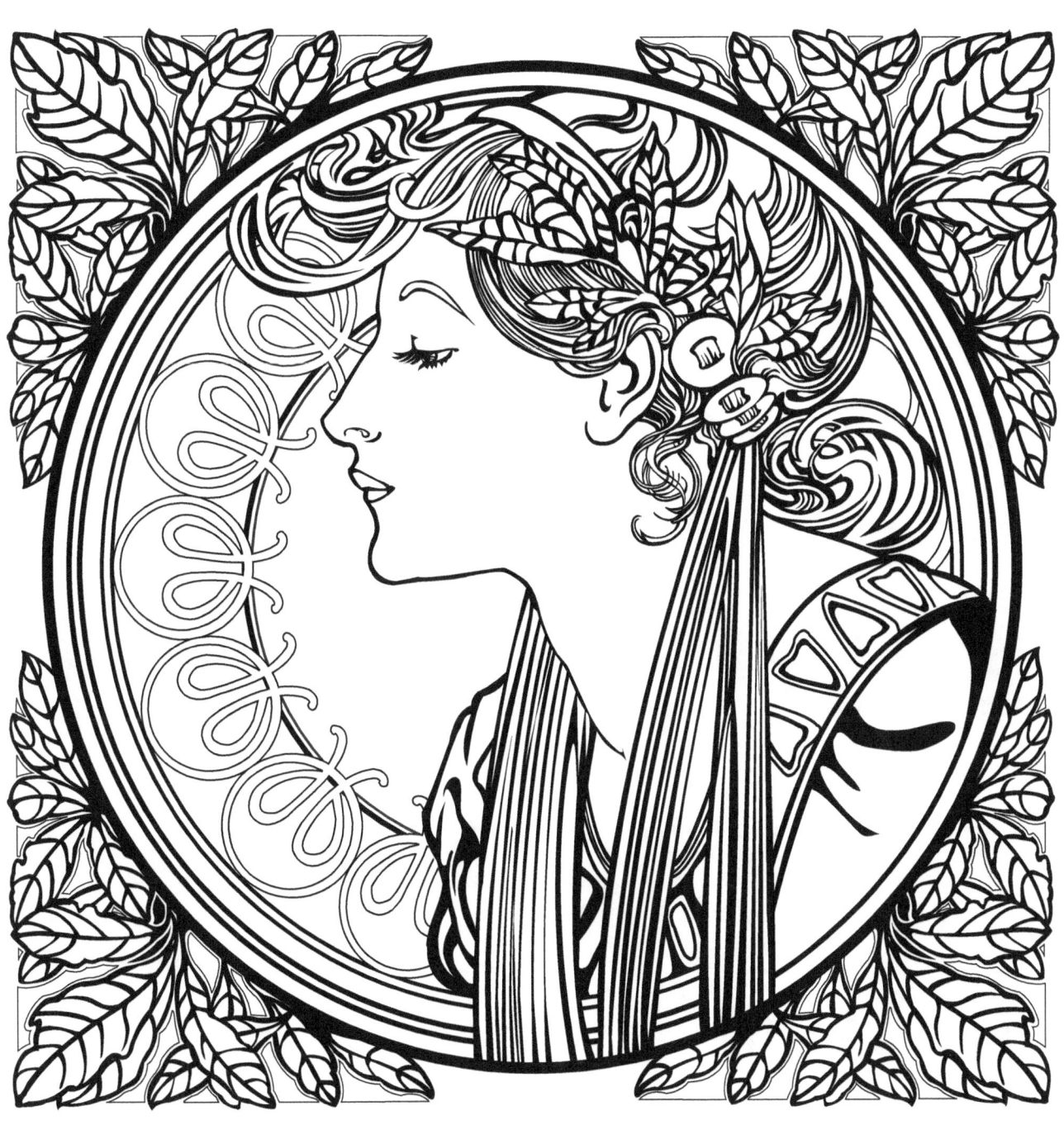

LAUREL, 1901 ALPHONSE MUCHA

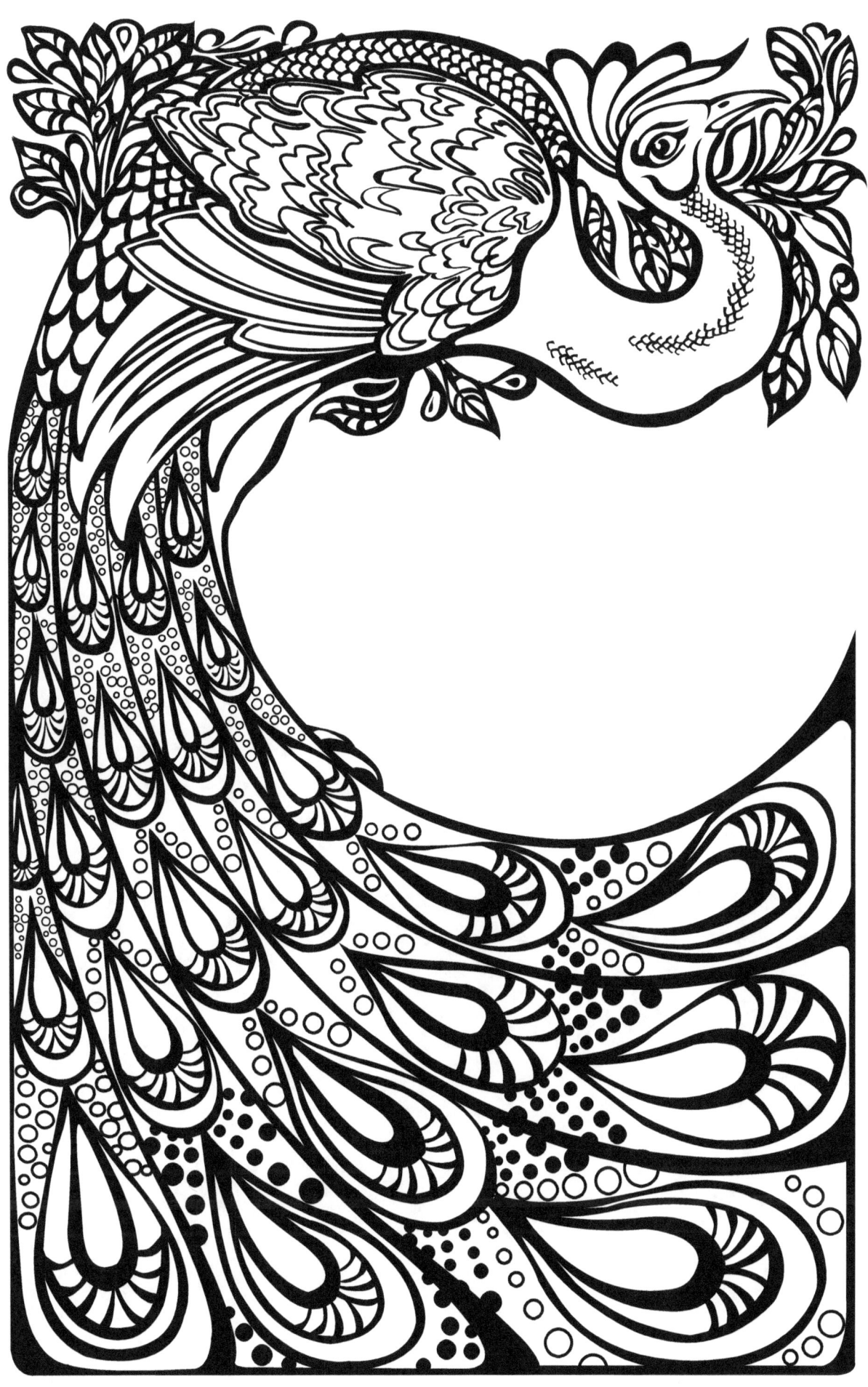

PEACOCK BOOK COVER, 1896 A. TURBAYNE

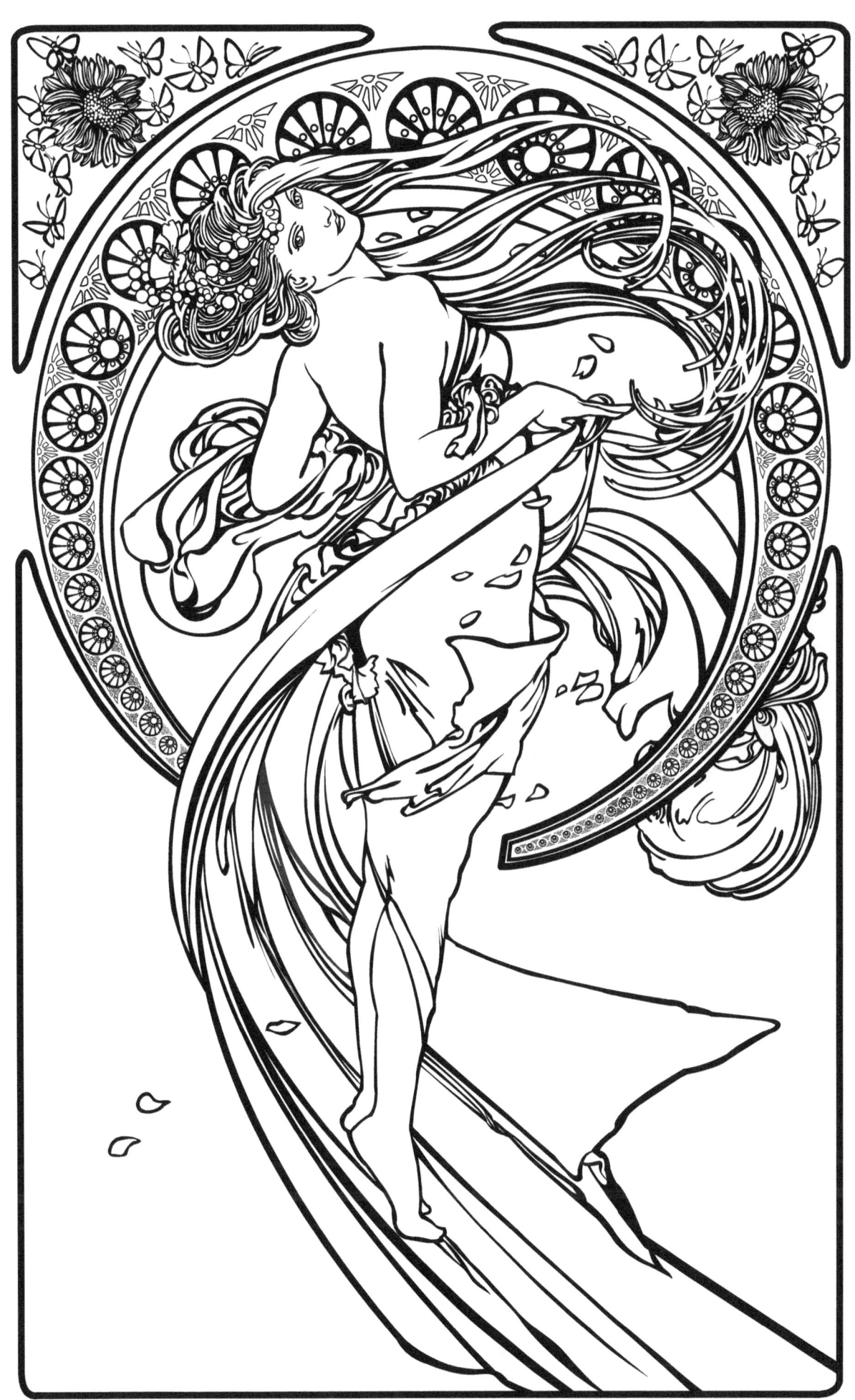

Dance, 1898 Alphonse Mucha

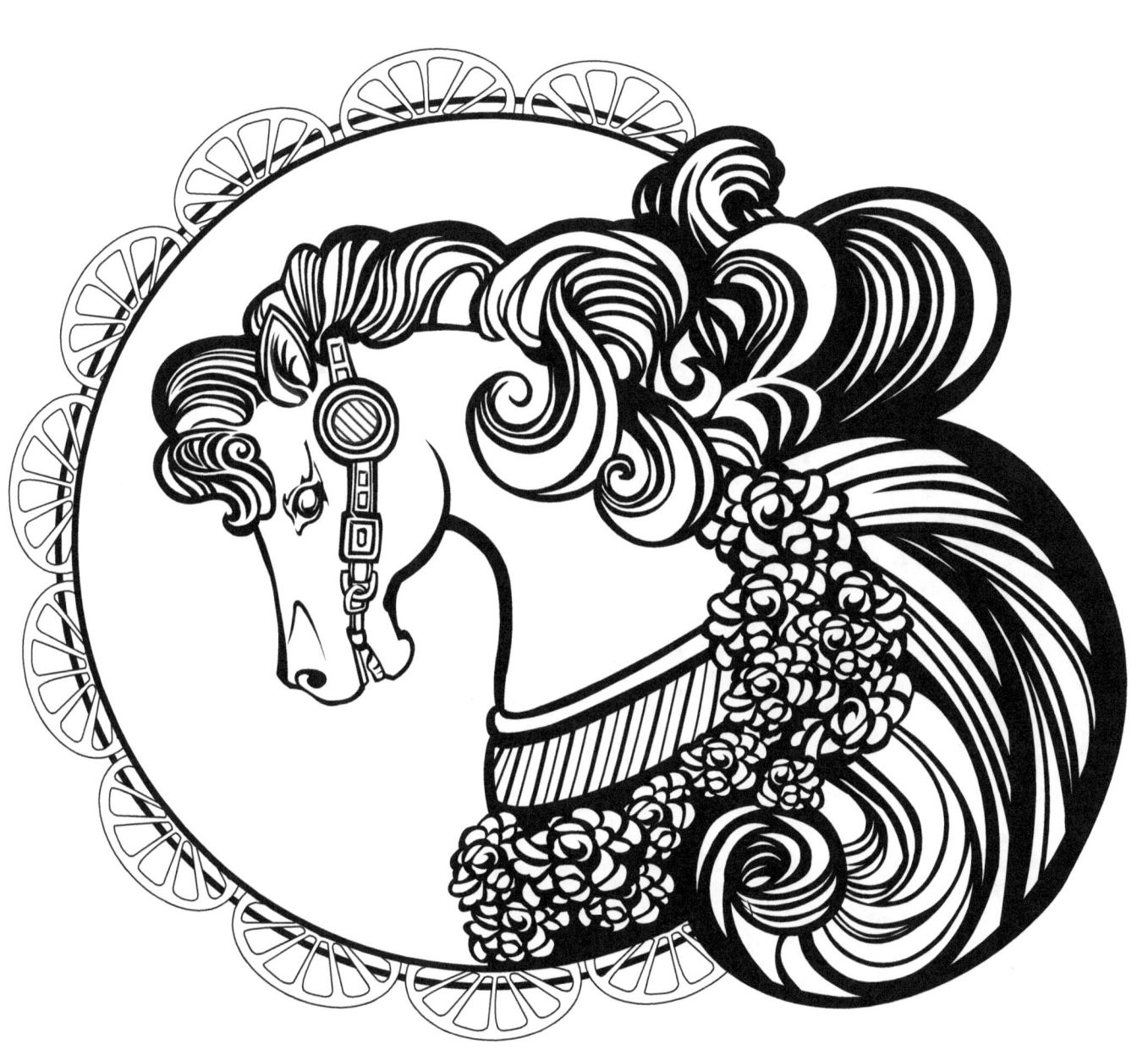

DAHLIA HORSE, 2015 JENNIFER KOZLANSKY

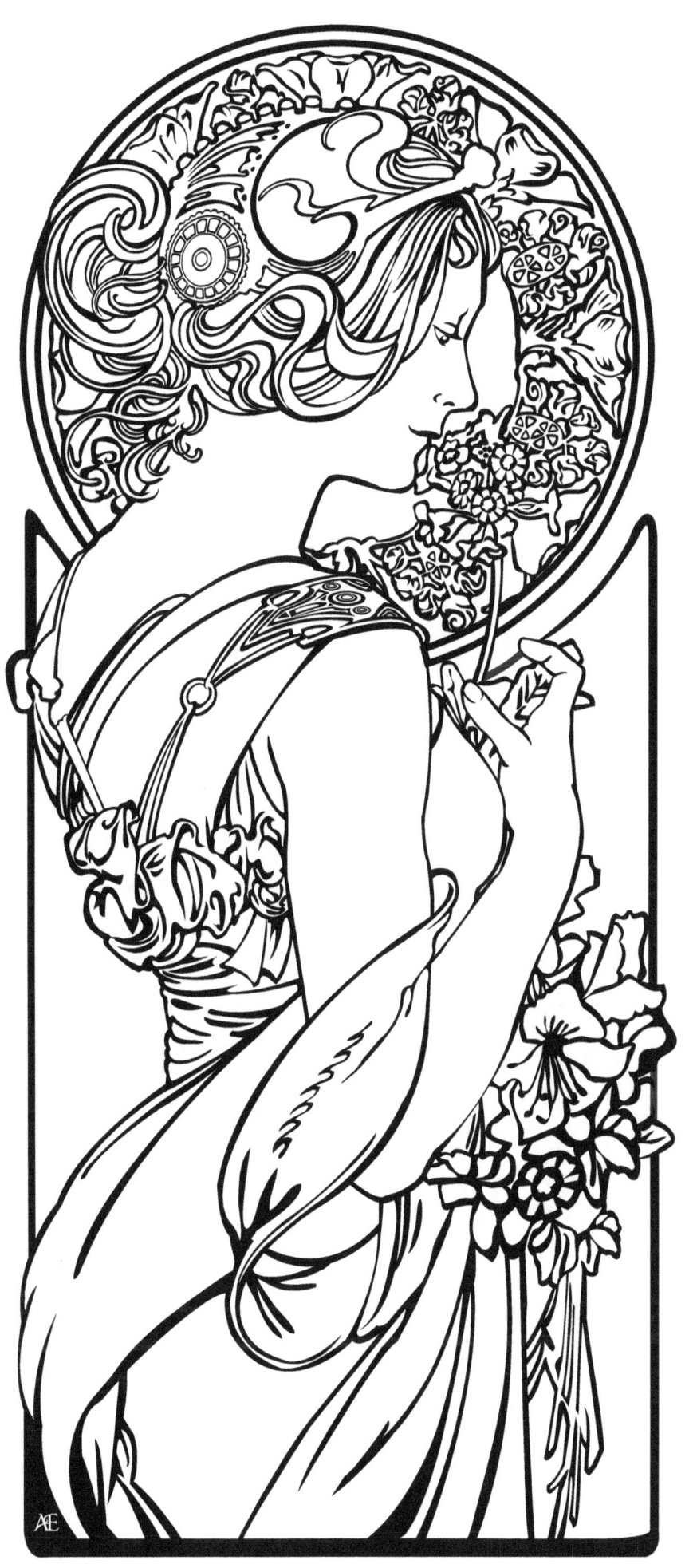

POLYANTHUS, 1899 ALPHONSE MUCHA

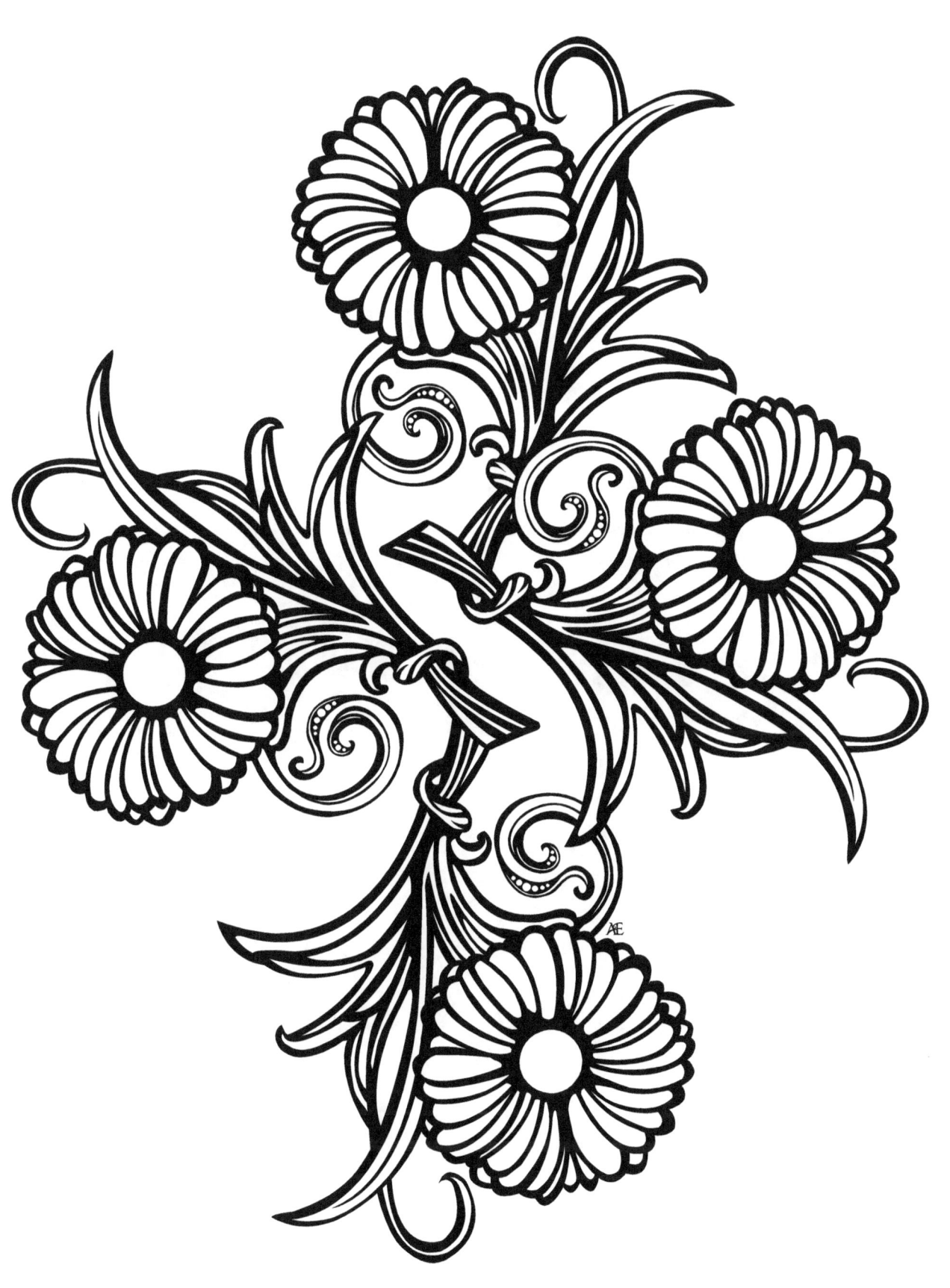

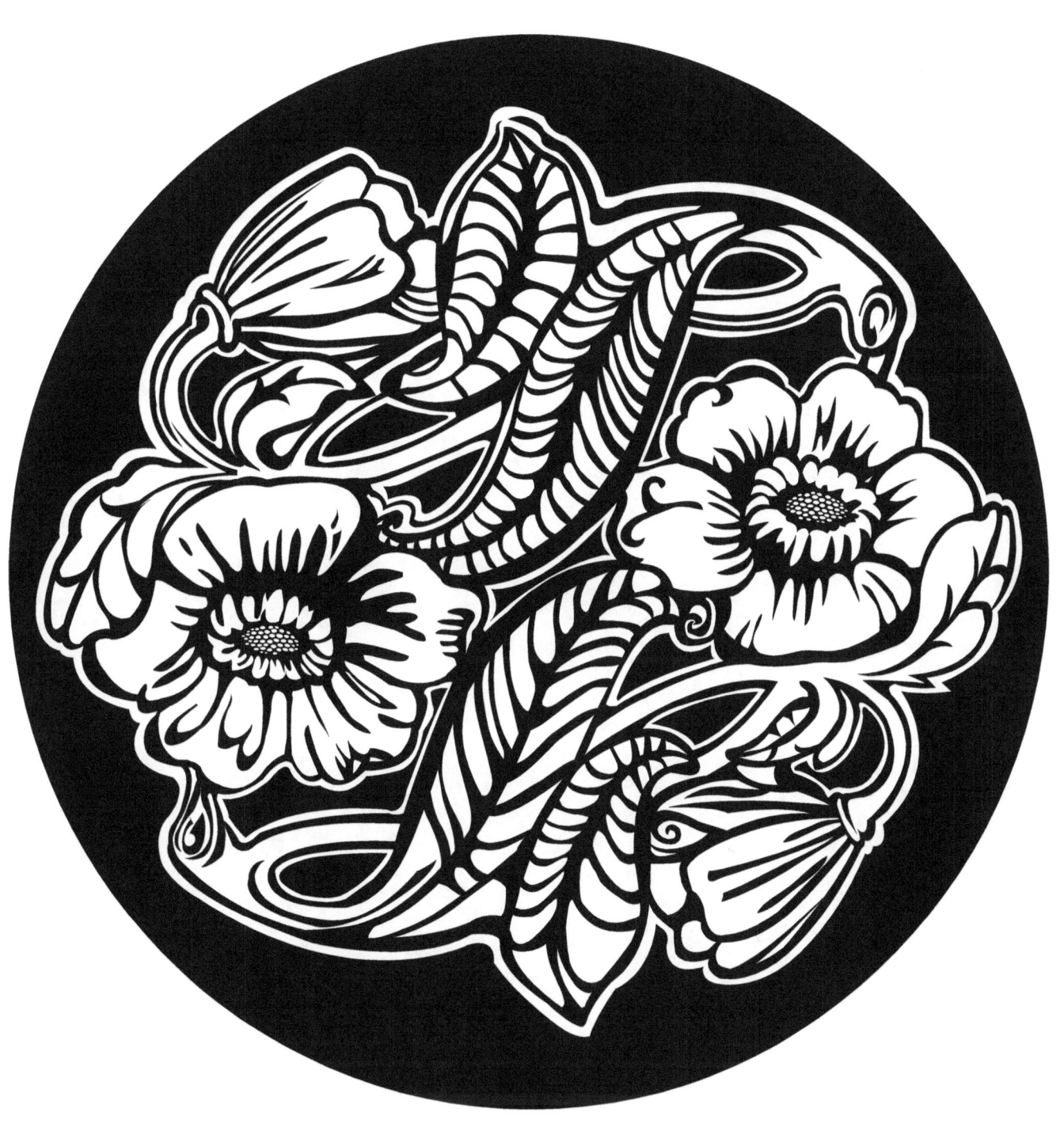

PRIMROSES, 2015 JENNIFER KOZLANSKY

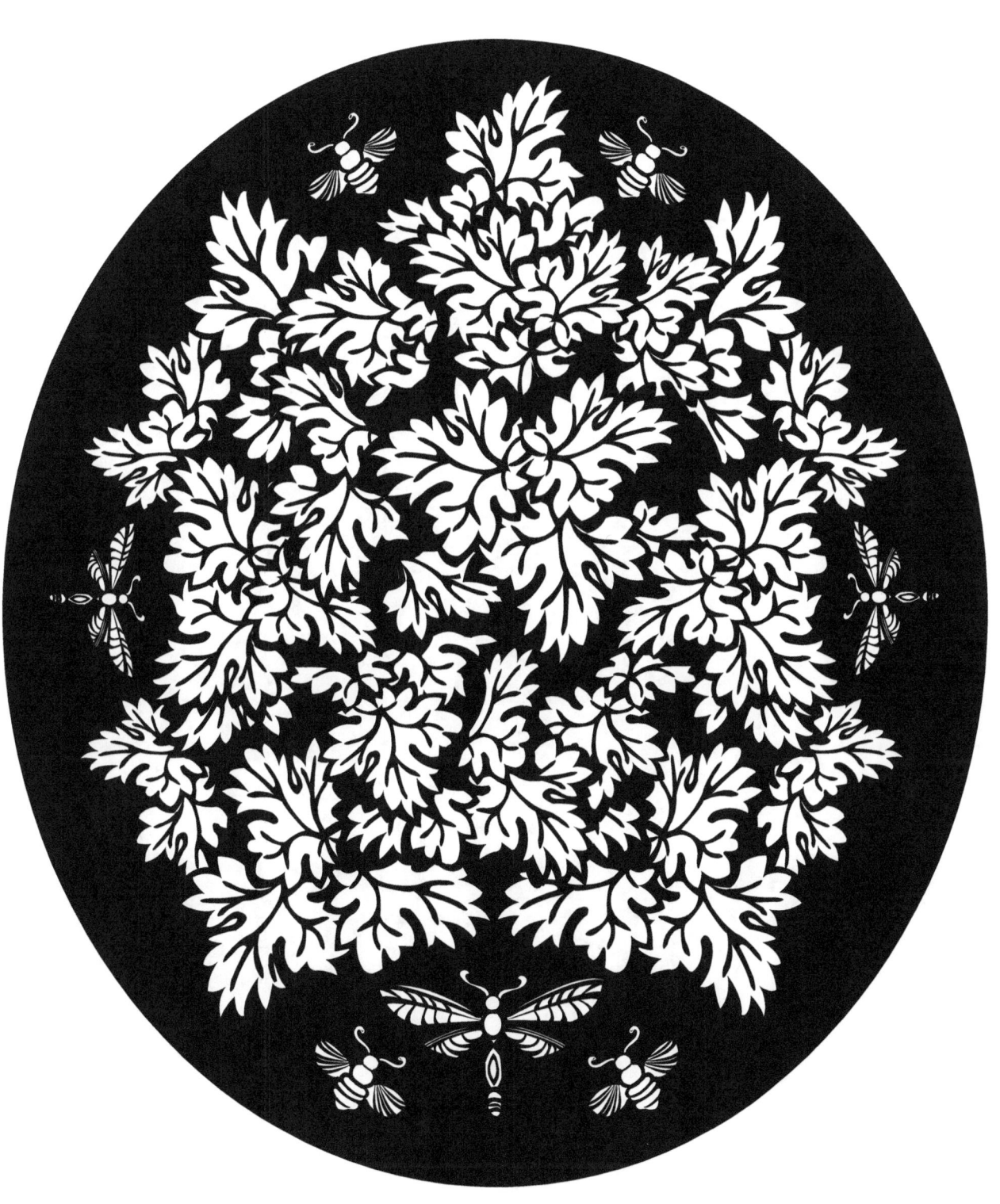

AUTUMN LEAVES, 2015 JENNIFER KOZLANSKY

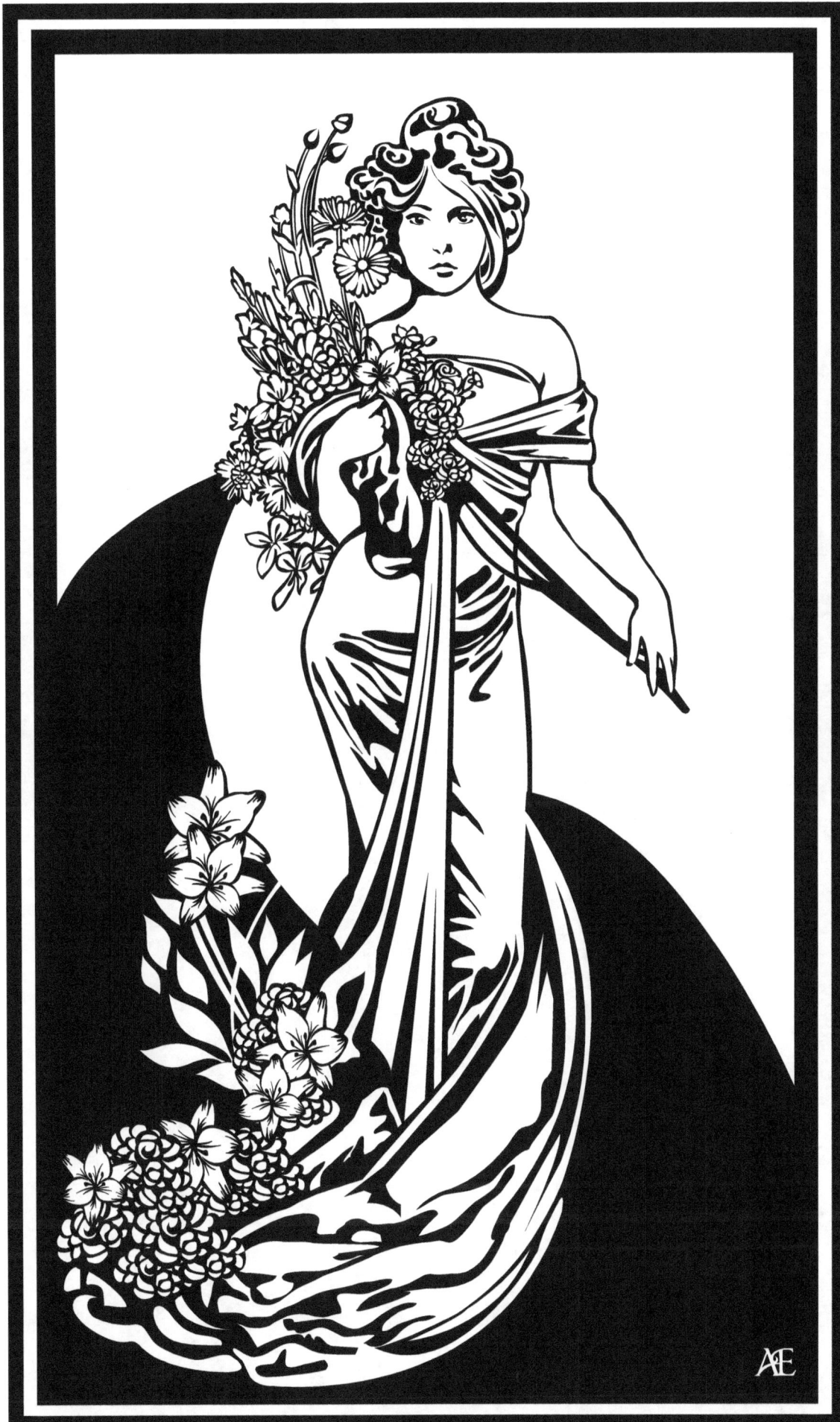

SPRING, 1900 ALPHONSE MUCHA

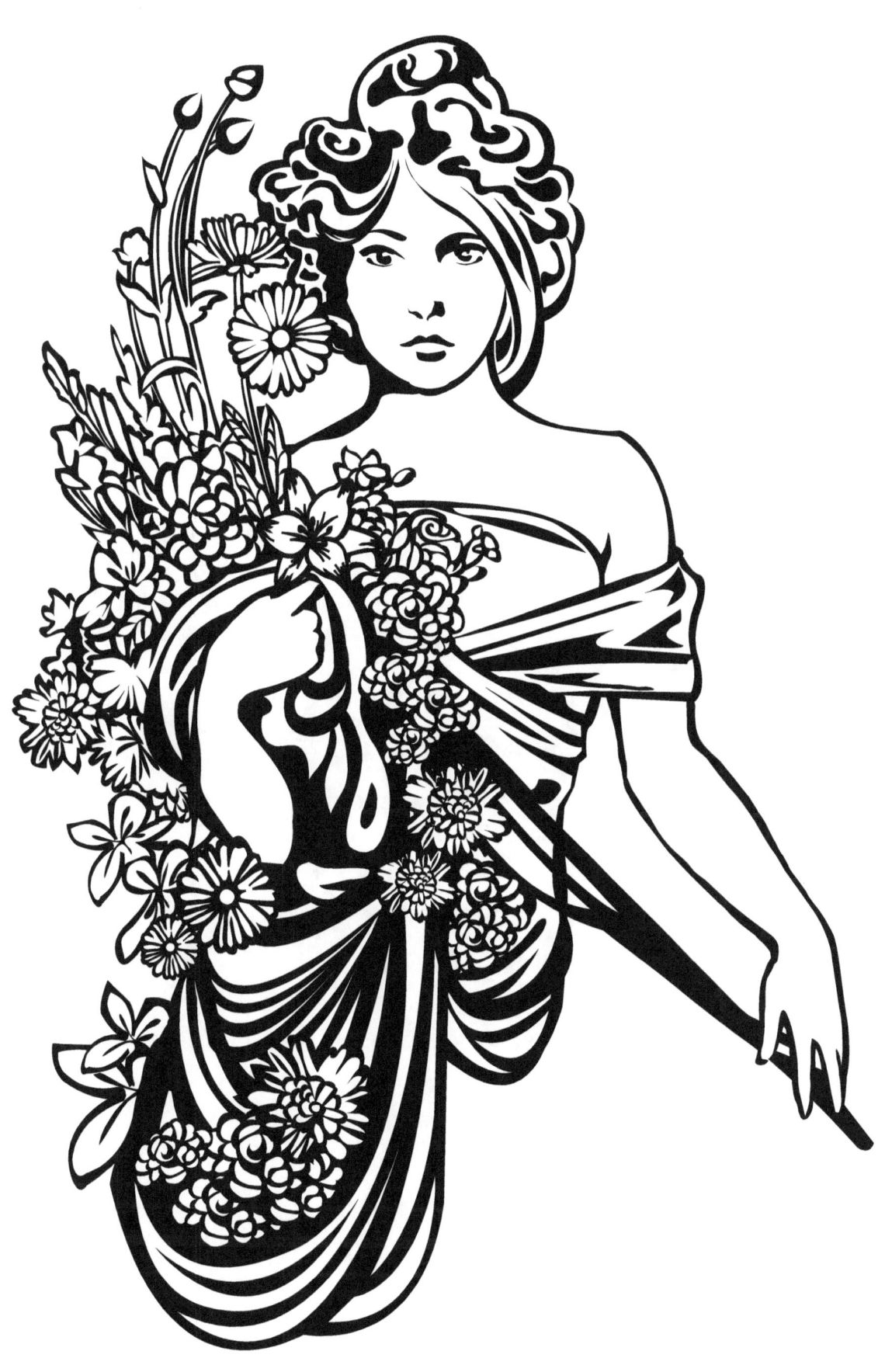

SPRING DETAIL 1900 ALPHONSE MUCHA

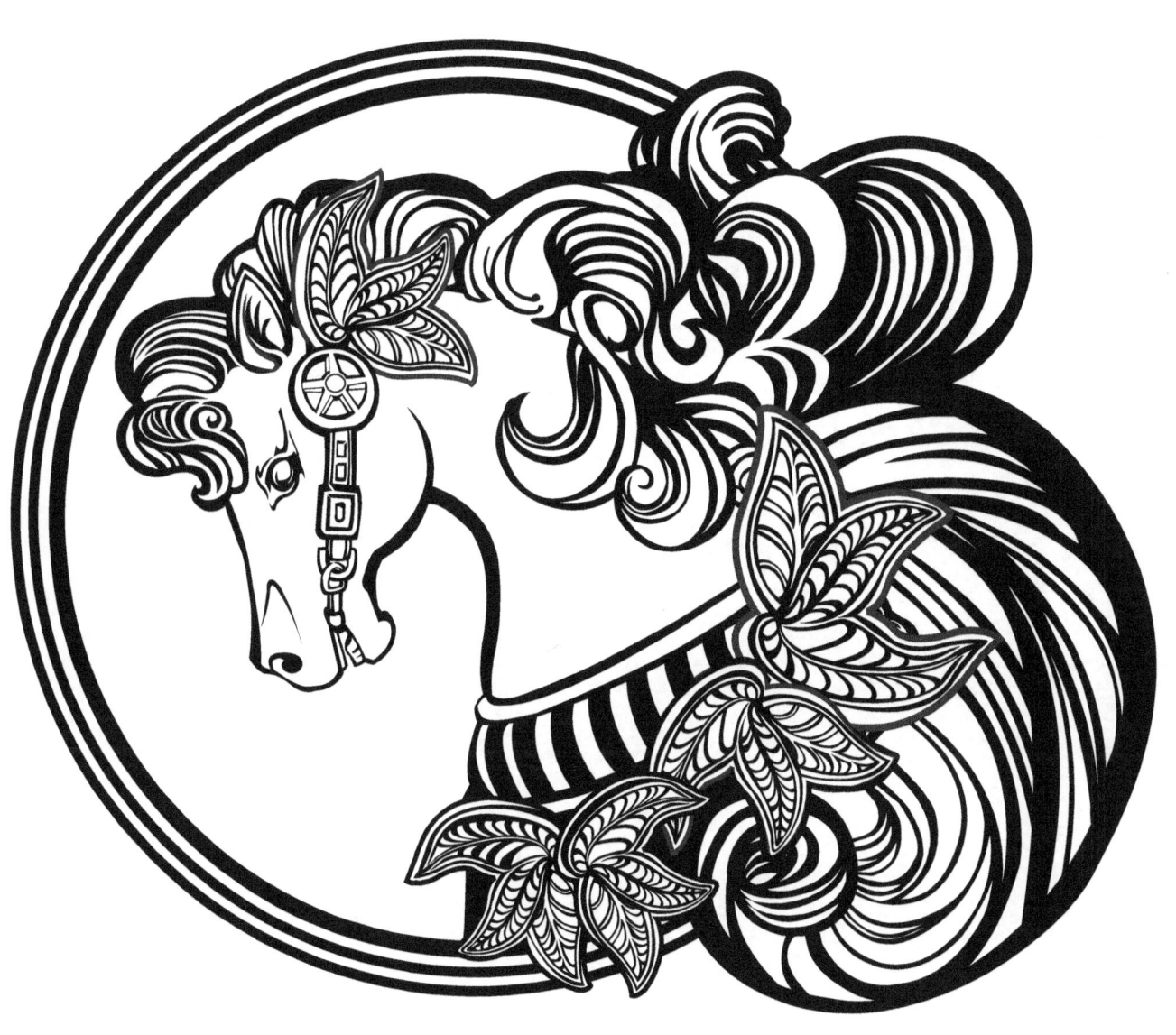

FROND HORSE 2015 JENNIFER KOZLANSKY

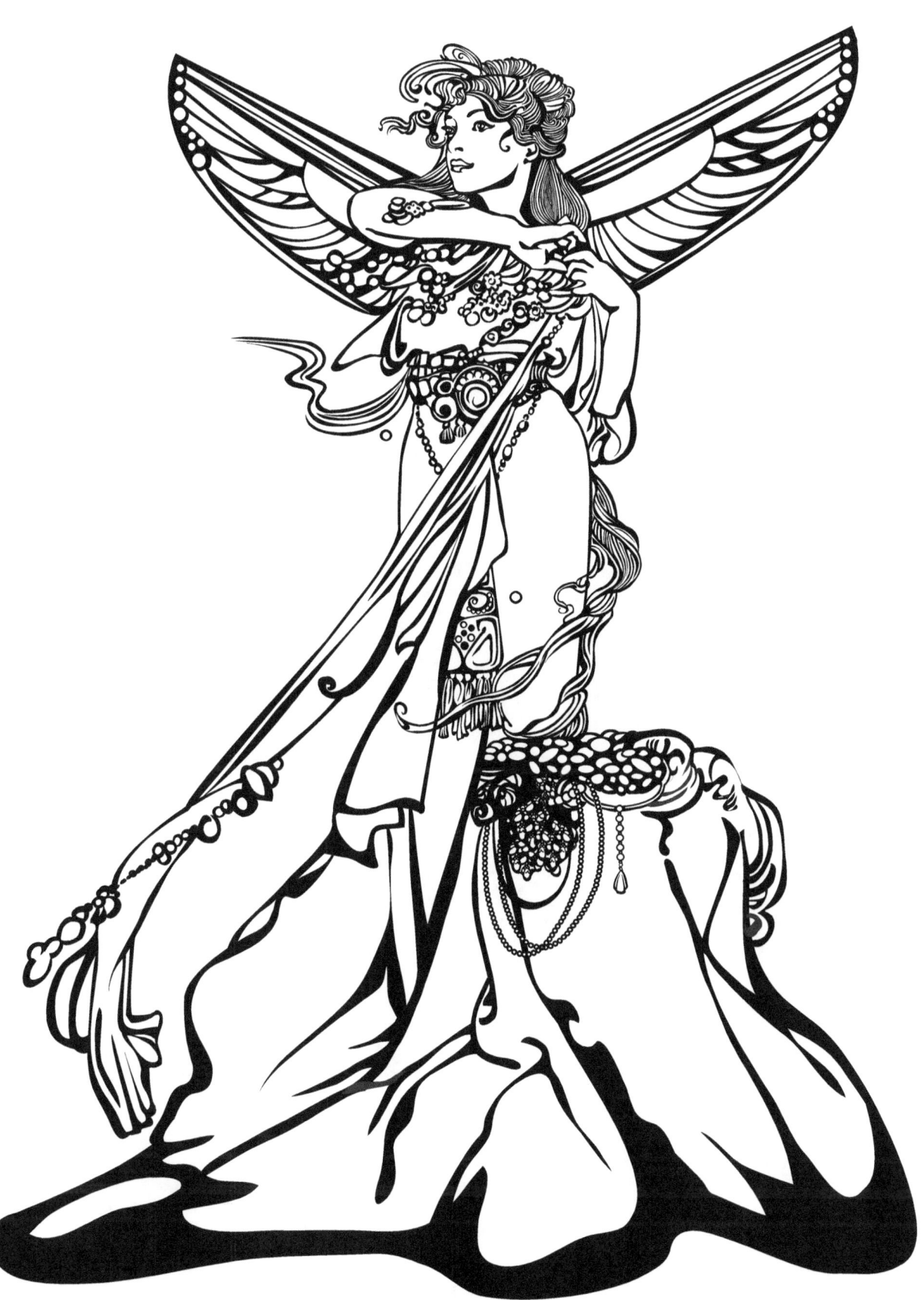

RAMA, 1898 ALPHONSE MUCHA

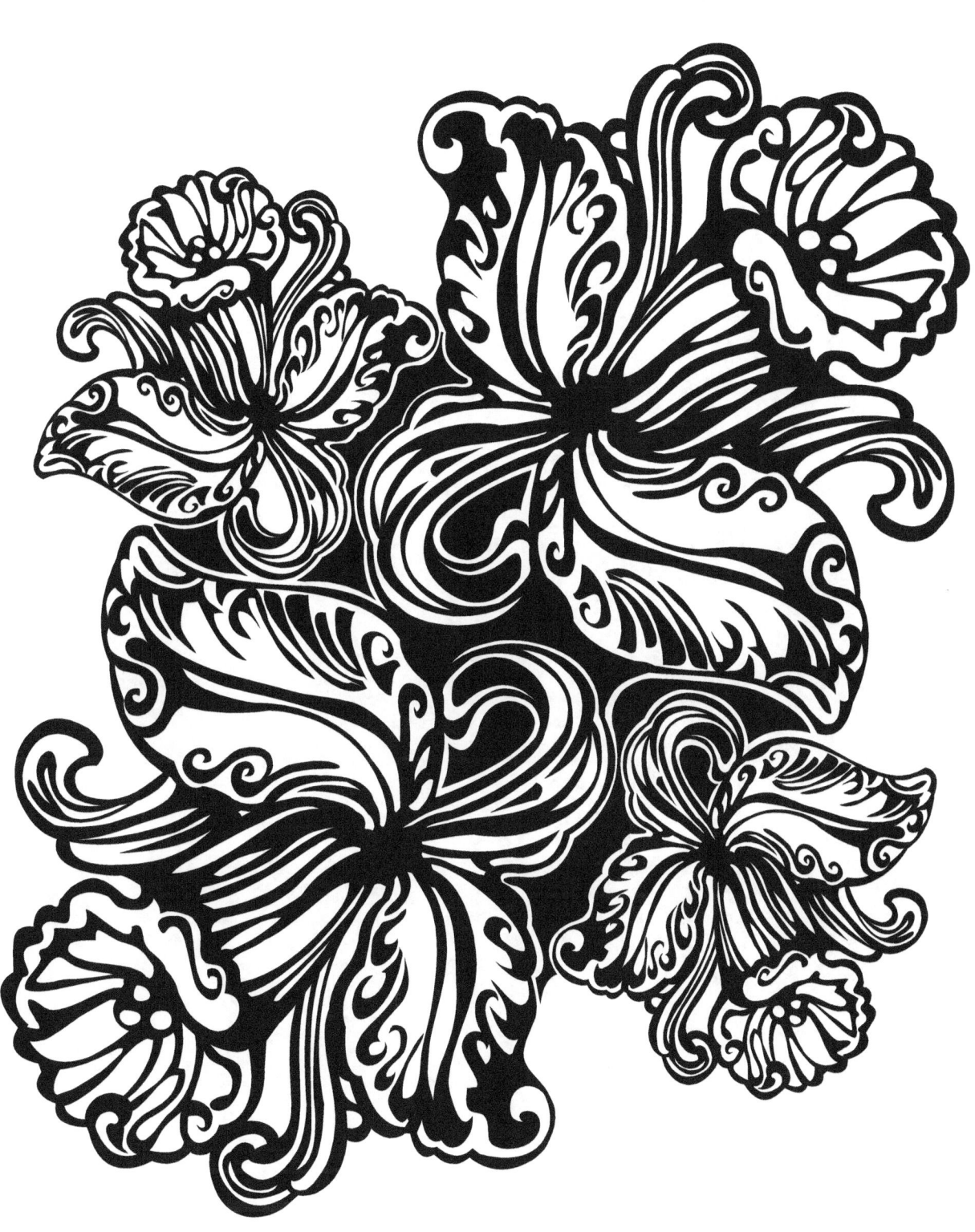

DAFFODILS, 2015 JENNIFER KOZLANSKY

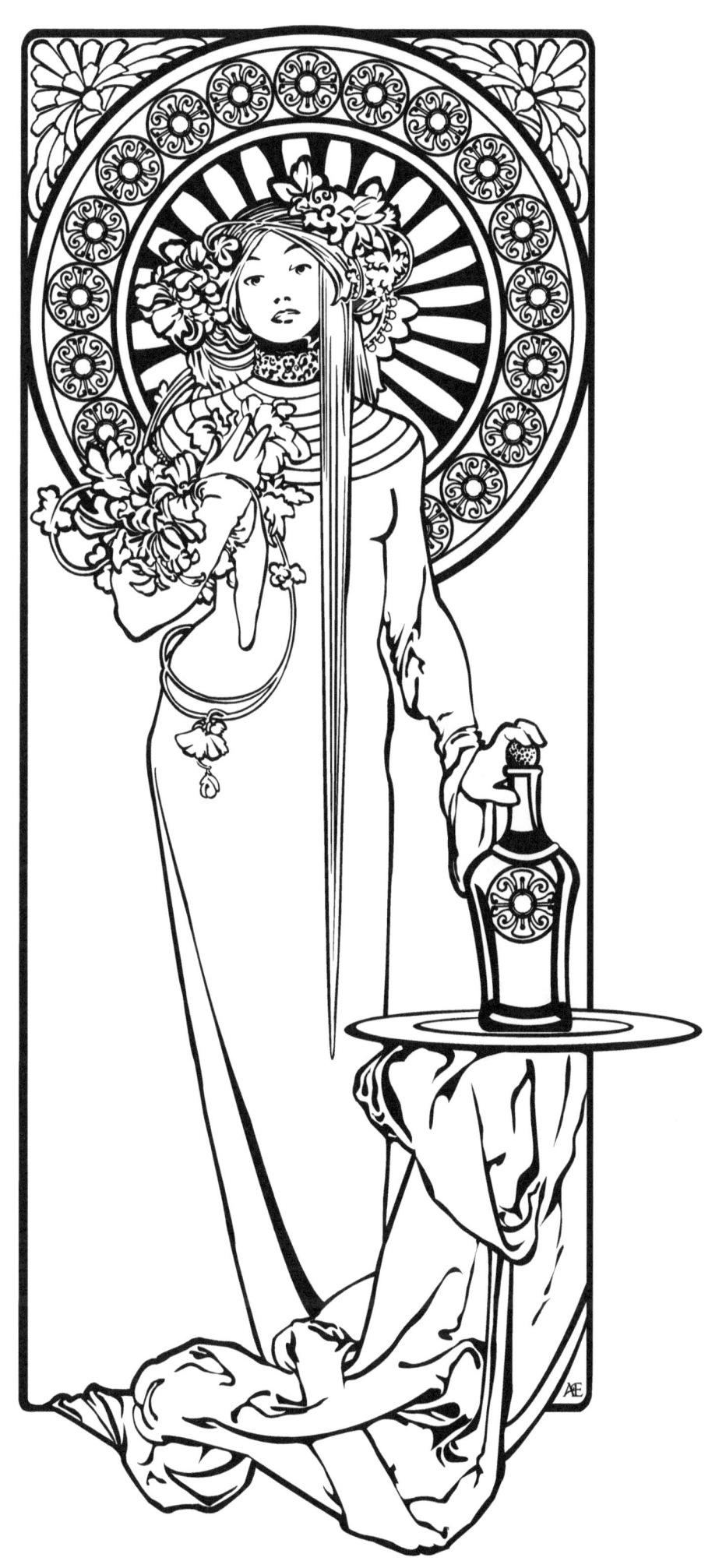

La Trappistine, 1897 Alphonse Mucha

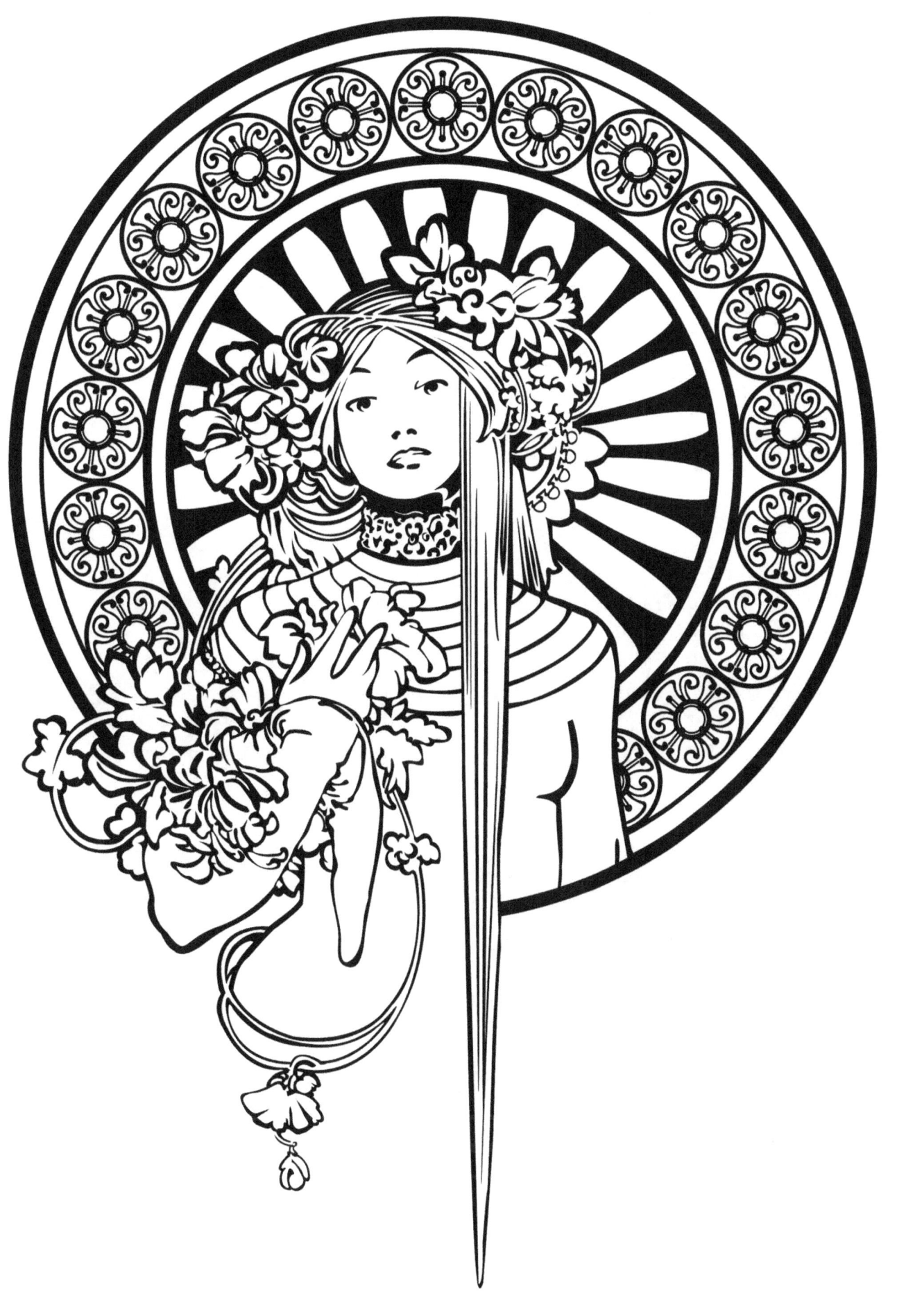

LA TRAPPISTINE DETAIL 1897 ALPHONSE MUCHA

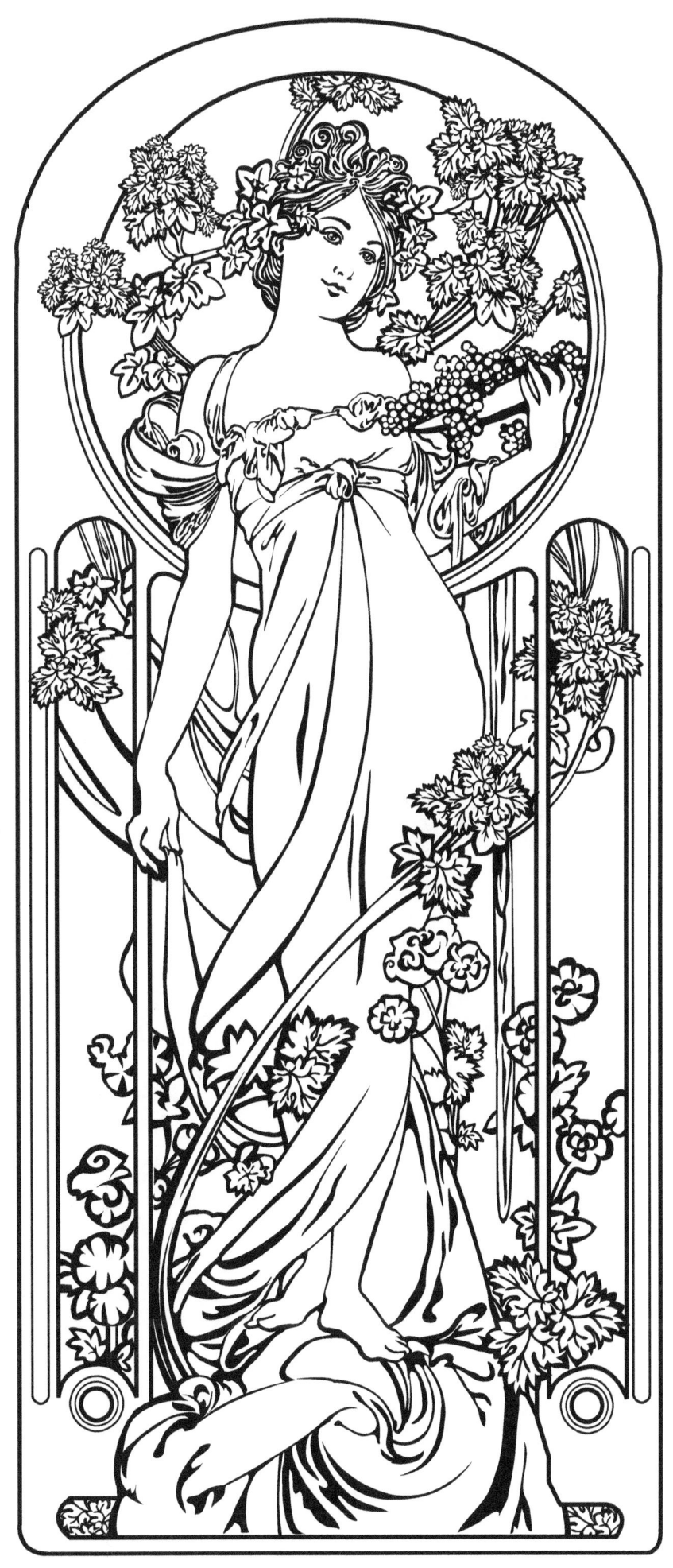

Champagne White Star, 1899 Mucha

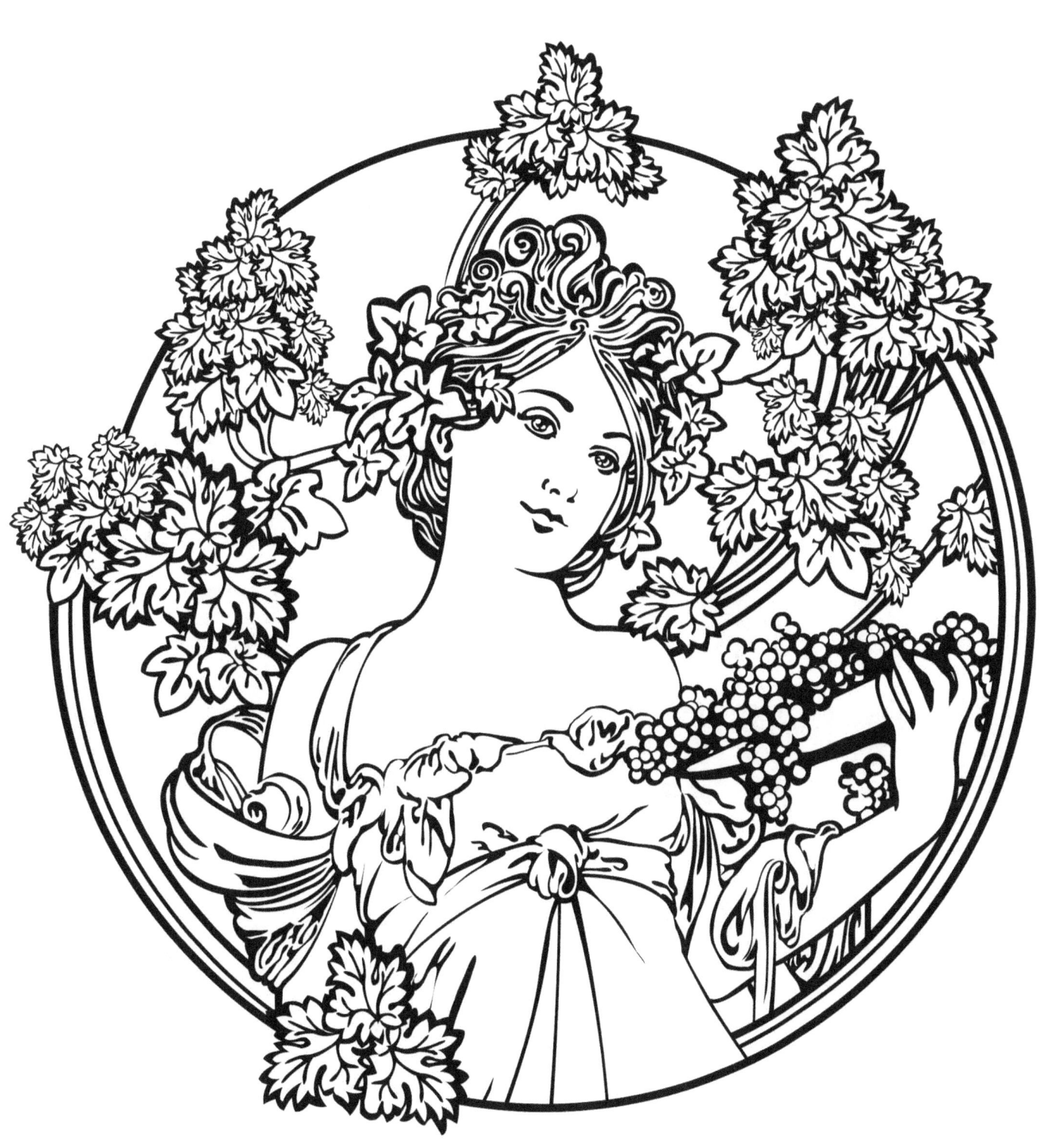

CHAMPAGNE WHITE STAR DETAIL, 1899 MUCHA

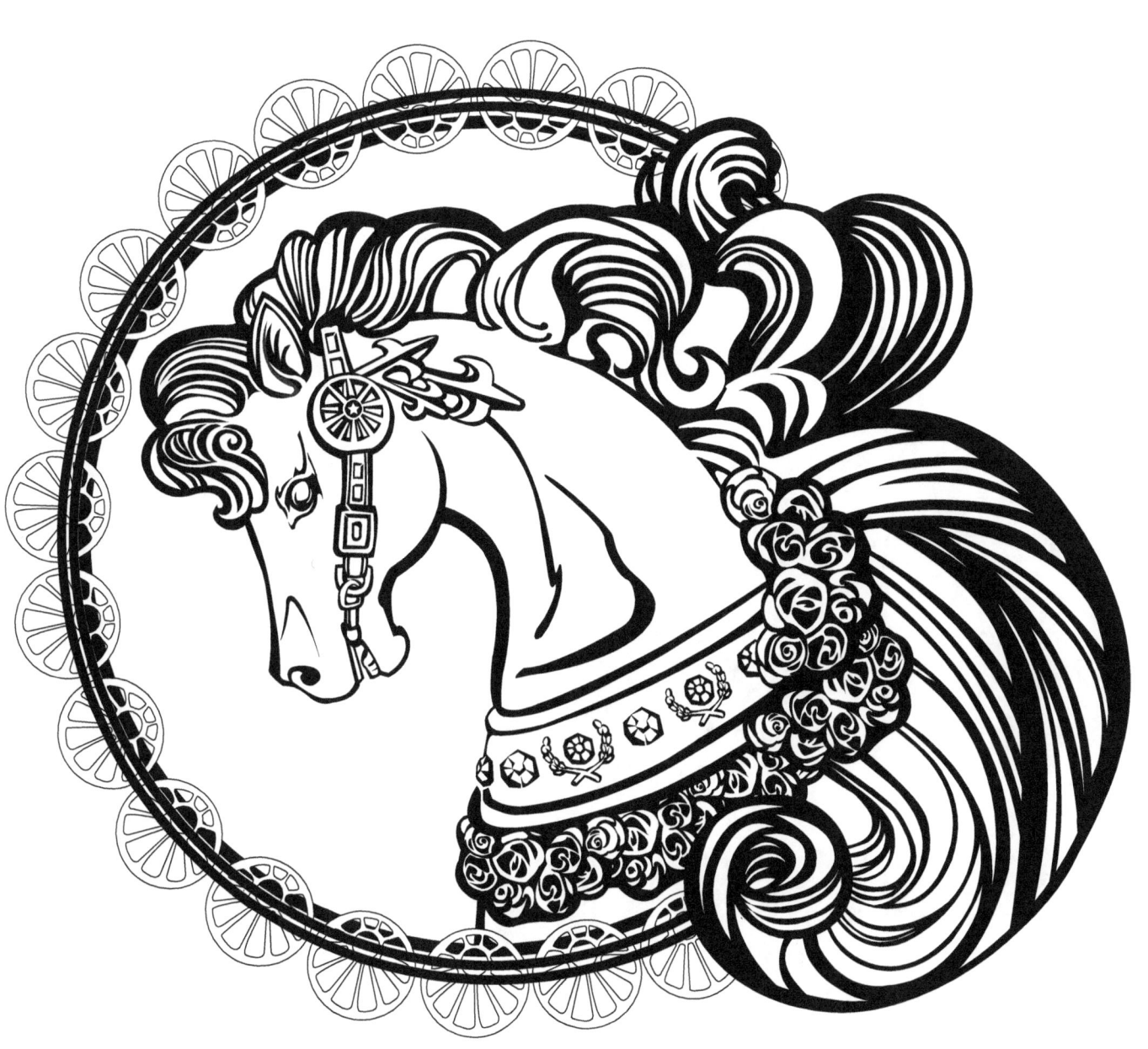

ROSE HORSE, 2015 JENNIFER KOZLANSKY

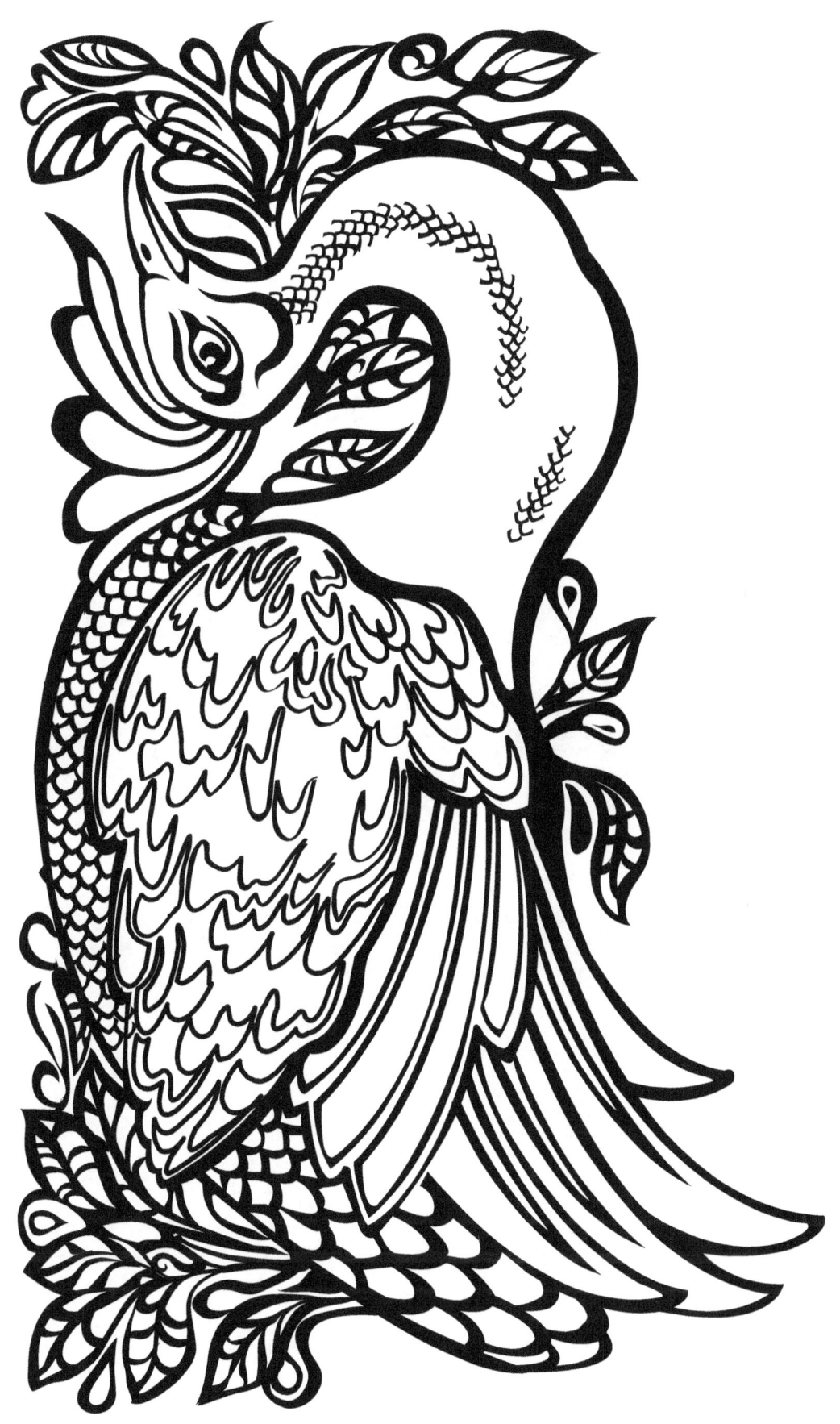

Peacock Detail 1896 A. Turbayne

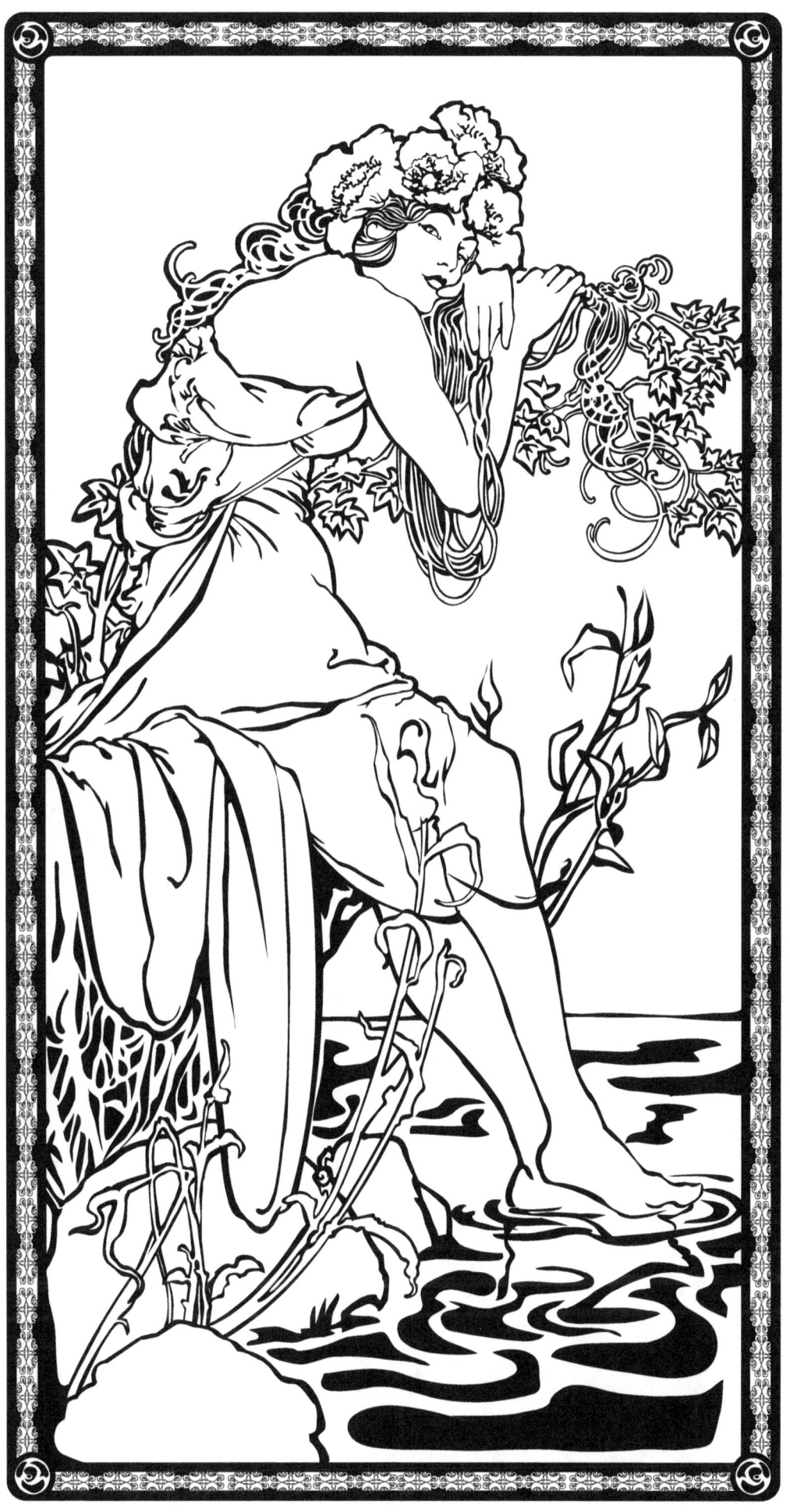

Summer, 1896 Alphonse Mucha

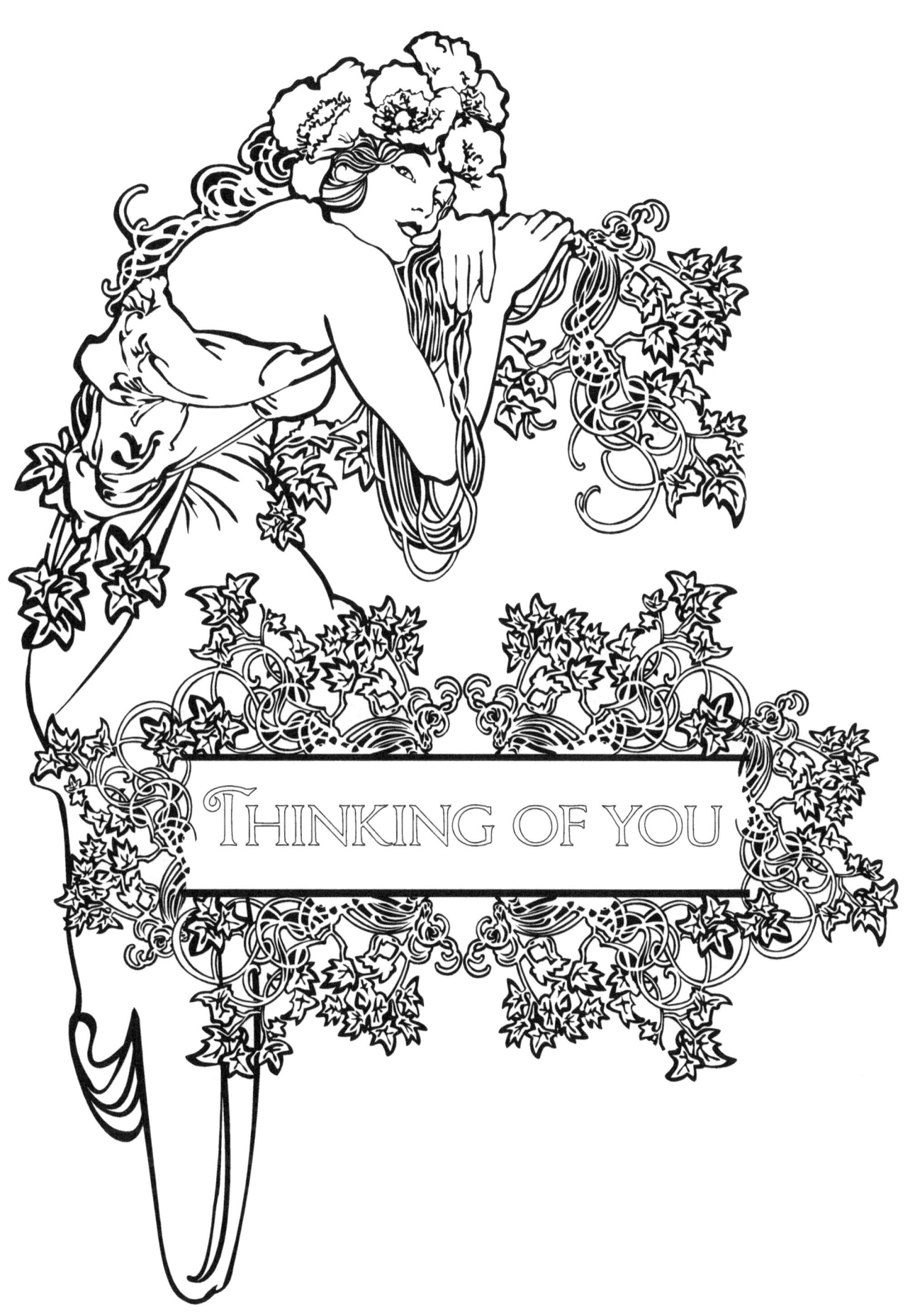

Thinking of You Sentiment Mucha/Kozlansky

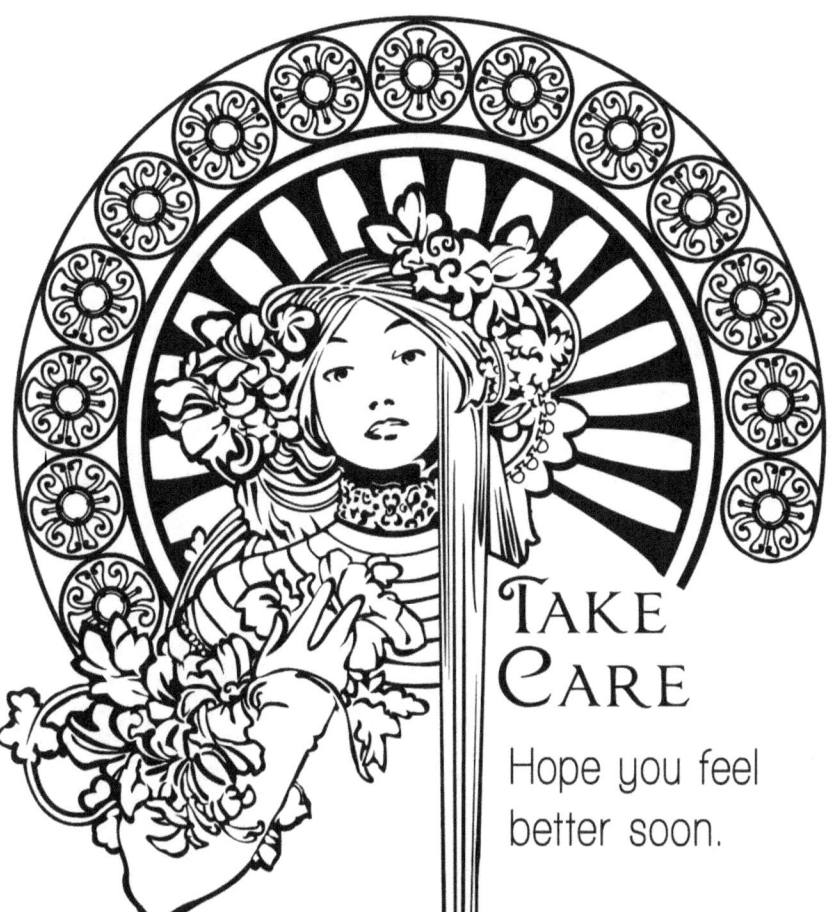

TAKE
CARE

Hope you feel
better soon.

Get Well Sentiment Mucha/Kozlansky

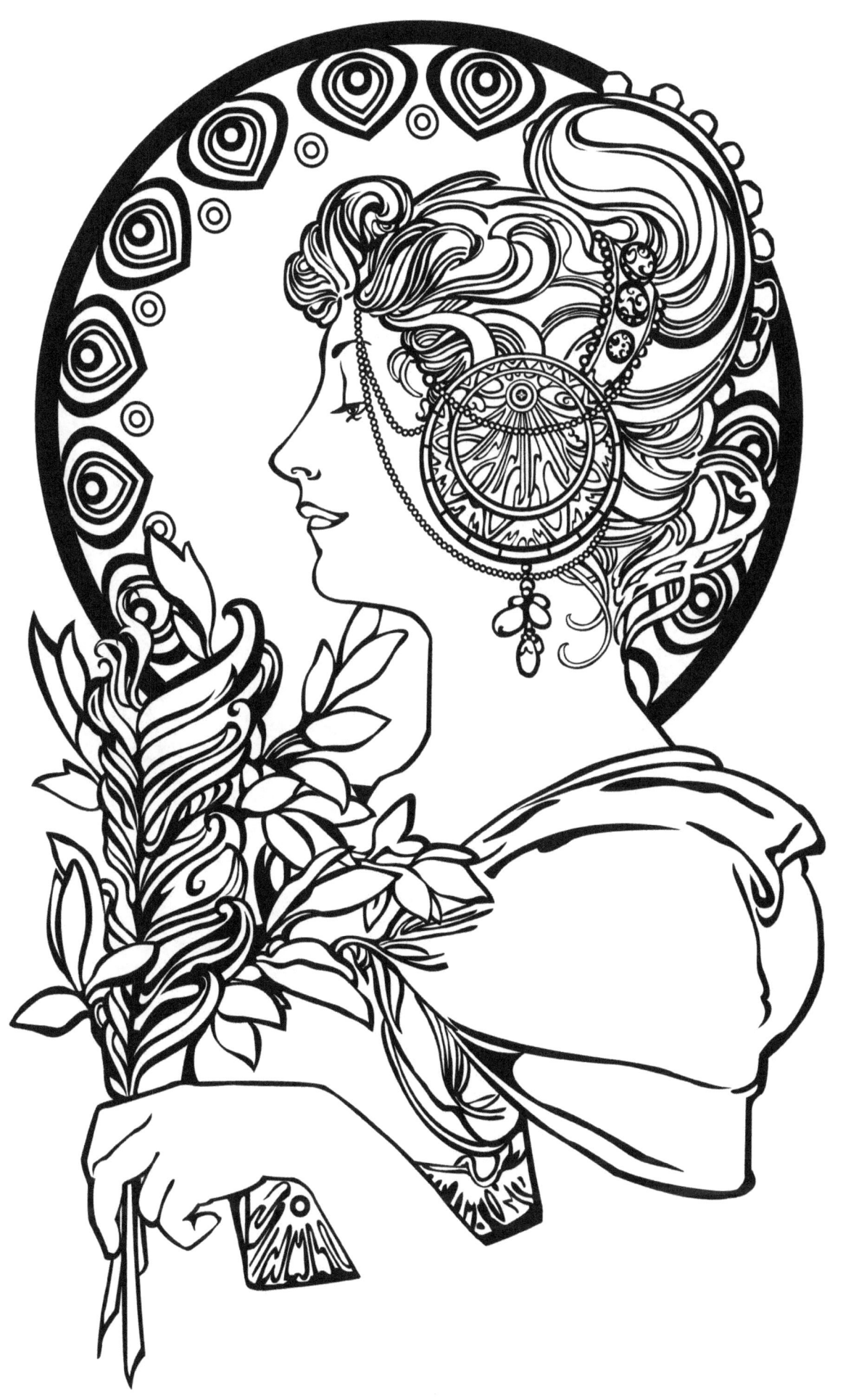

La Plume Detail 1899 Alphonse Mucha

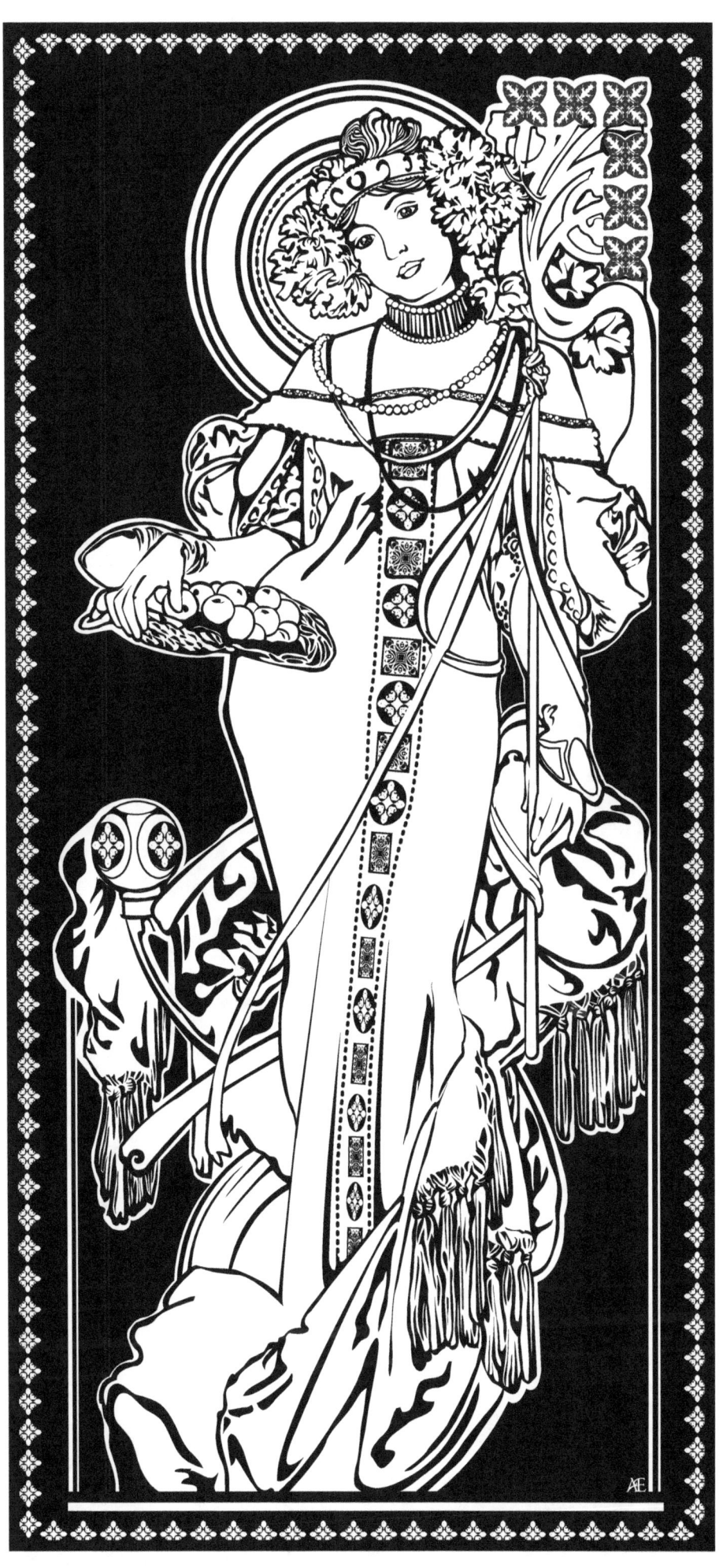

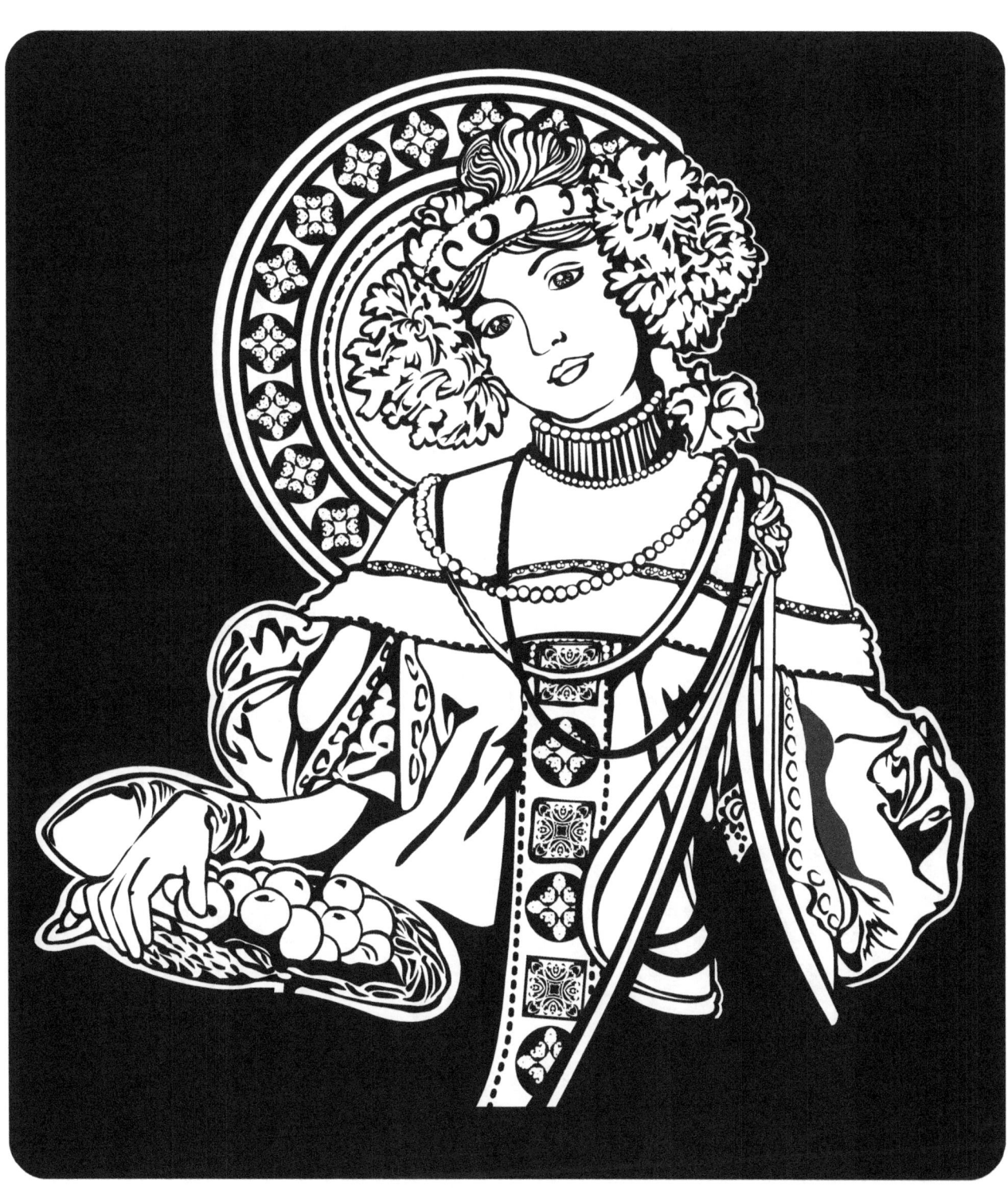

Autumn Detail 1899 Alphonse Mucha

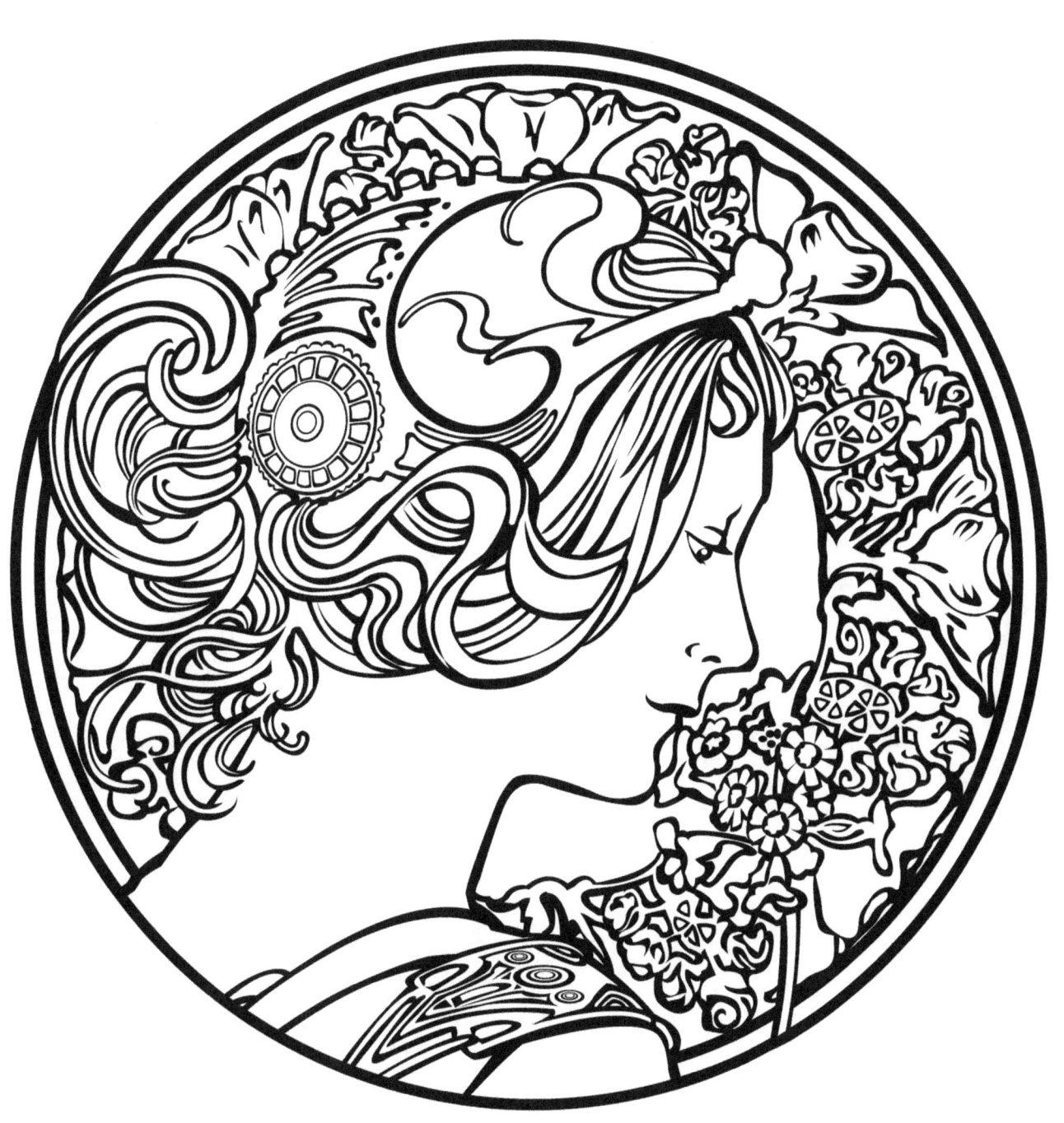

POLYANTHUS DETAIL 1899 ALPHONSE MUCHA

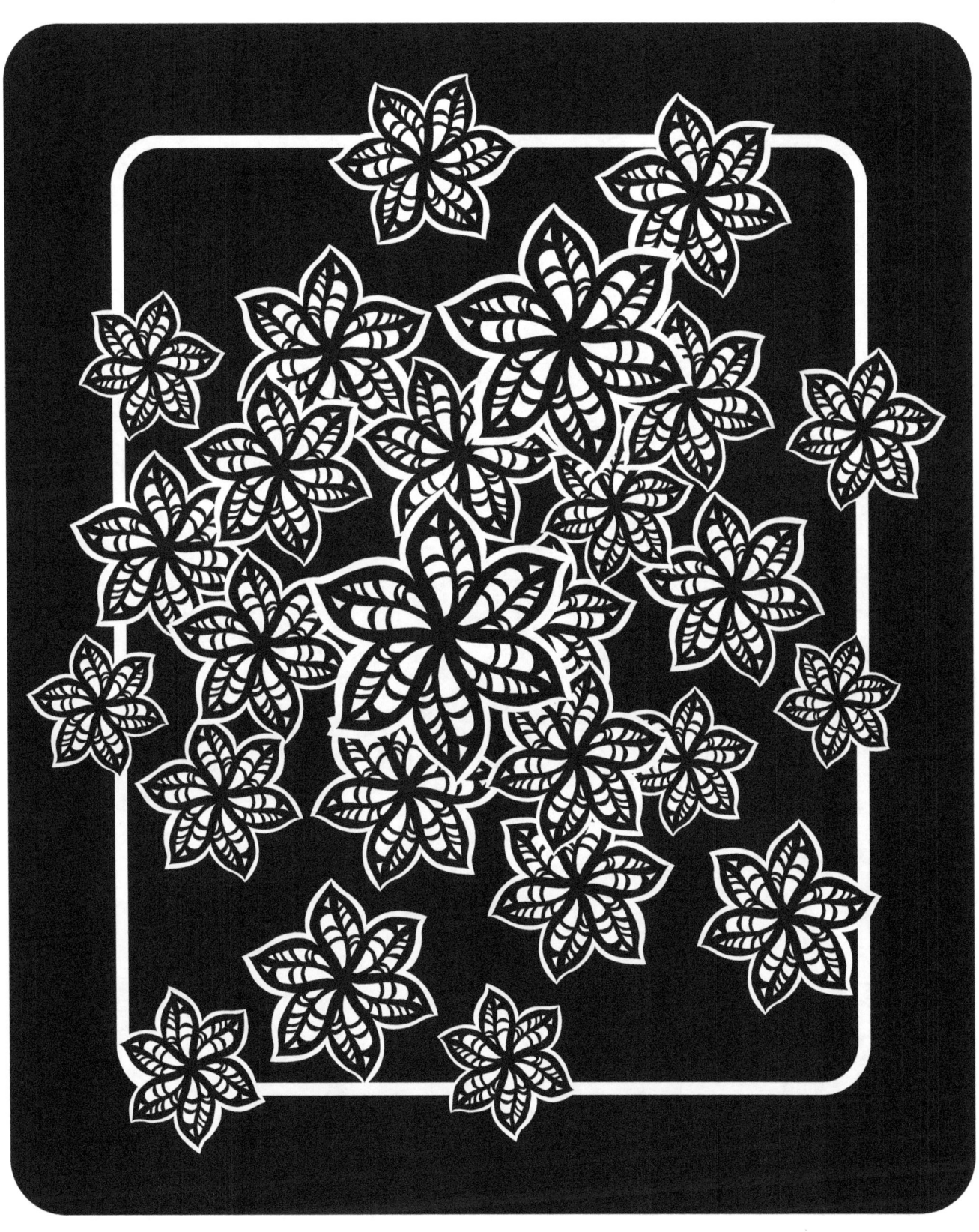

FLOWERS 2015 JENNIFER KOZLANSKY

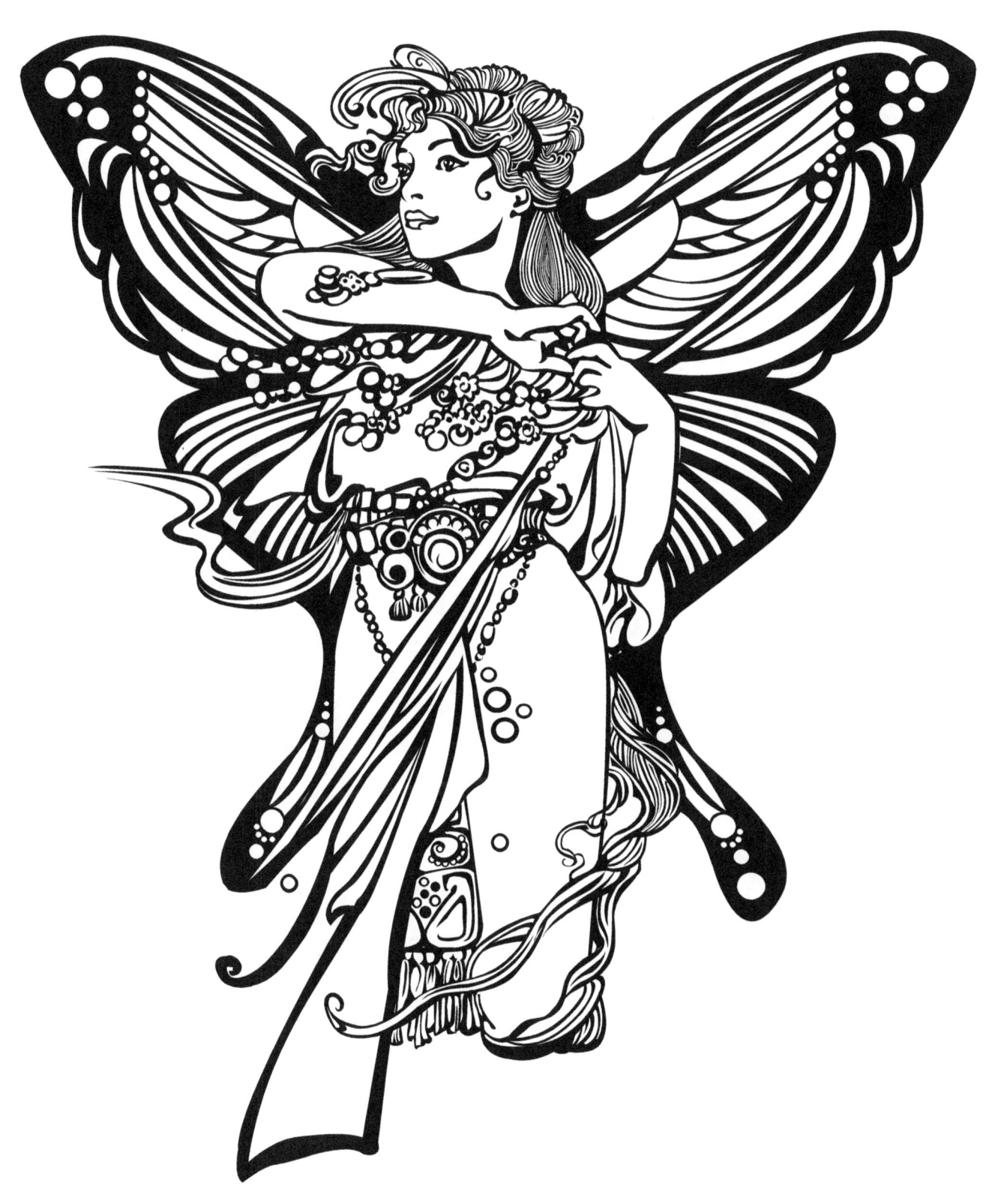

RAMA "BUTTERFLY" 1899 MUCHA/KOZLANSKY

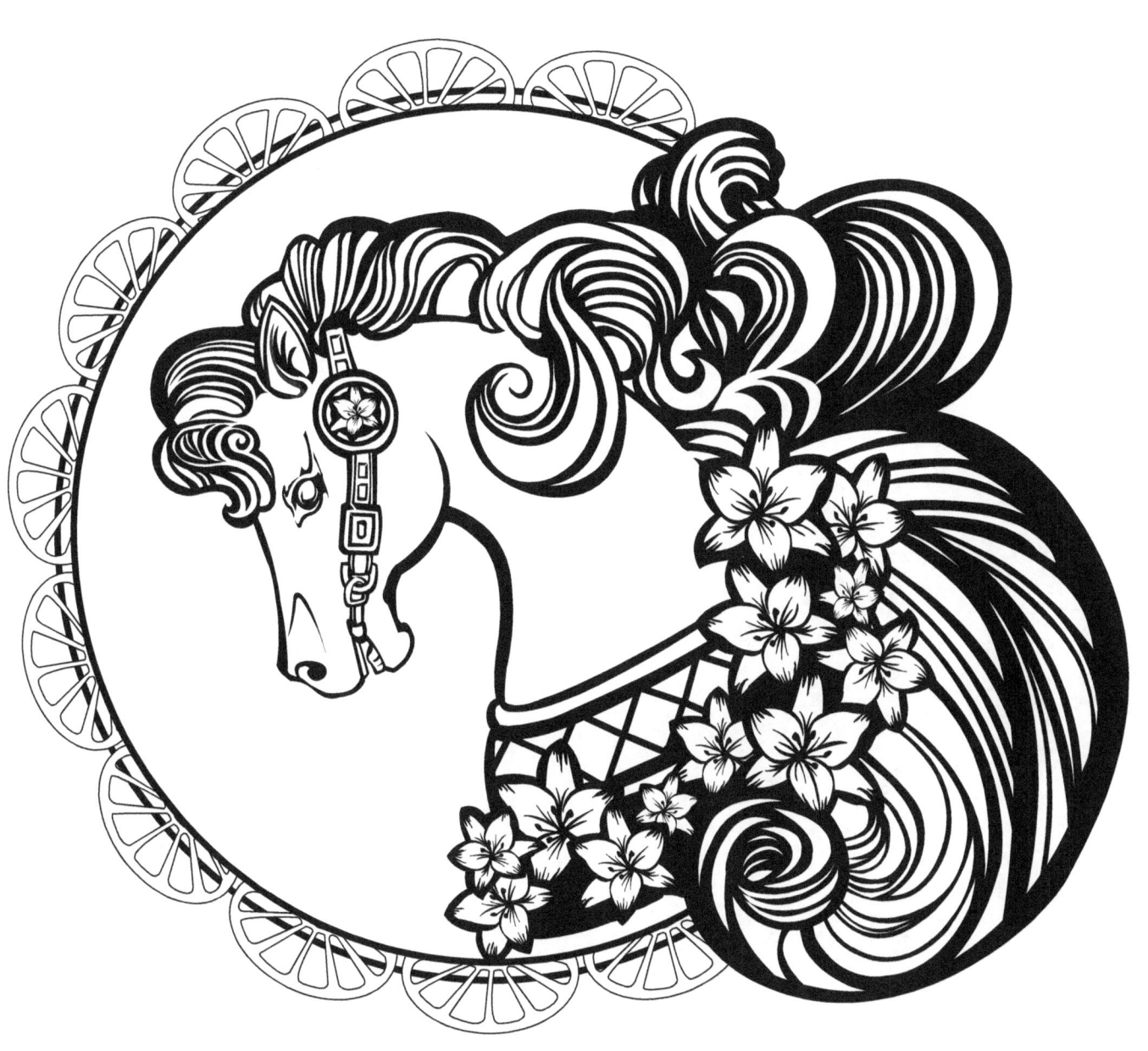

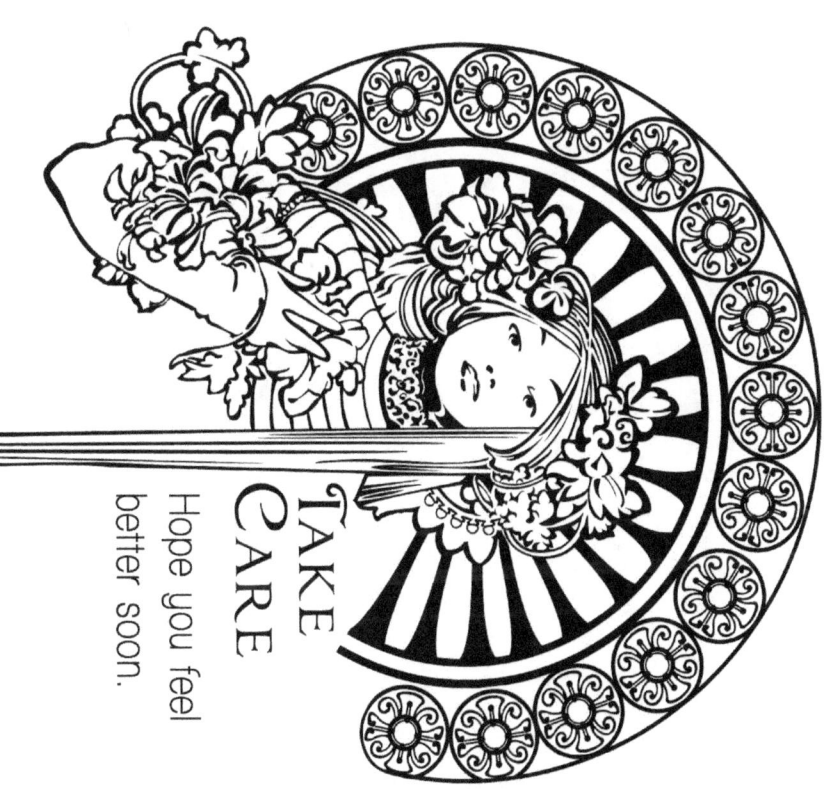

TAKE
CARE

Hope you feel
better soon.

GET WELL CARD MUCHA/KOZLANSKY

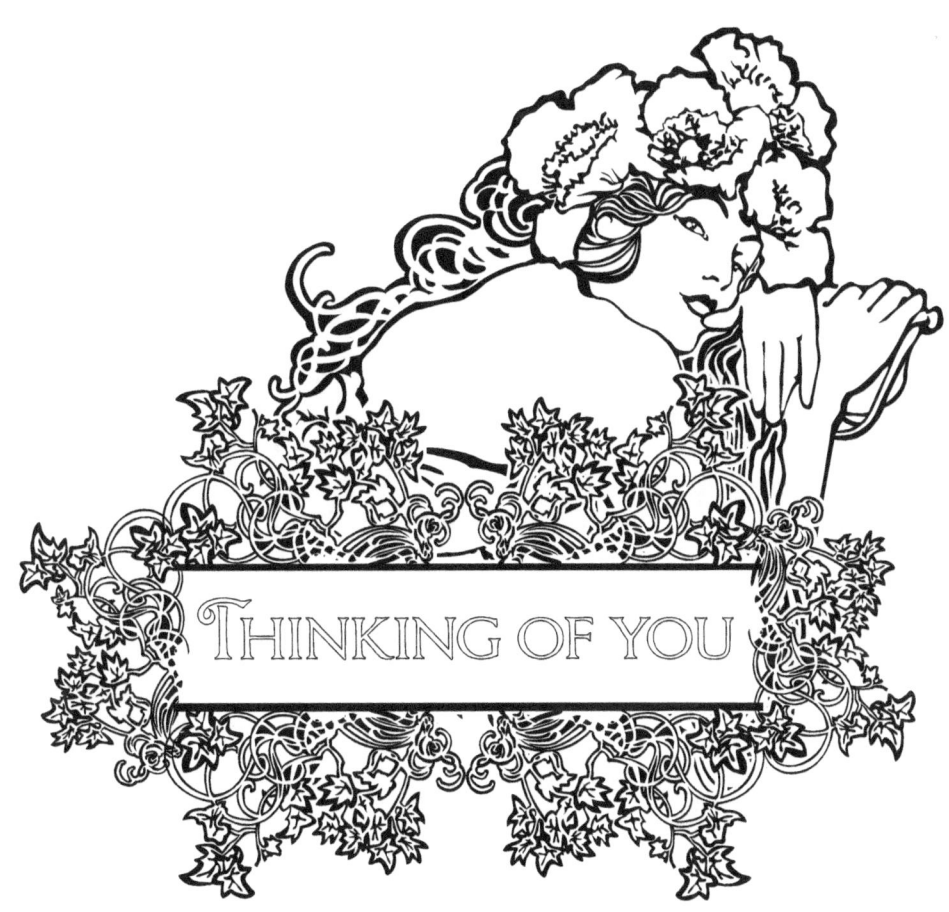

THINKING OF YOU

Thinking of You Card Mucha/Kozlansky

Fine Art
Coloring Group

Join the **Fine Art Coloring Group** to
share your work, give advice, get tips,
enter contests, and have access to
exclusive downloadable coloring sheets.

Do you love the greeting cards?
Join our Facebook group to download
perfectly formatted greeting card PDF files
that print out crisp and aligned on your
paper of choice.

facebook.com/groups/fineartcoloring

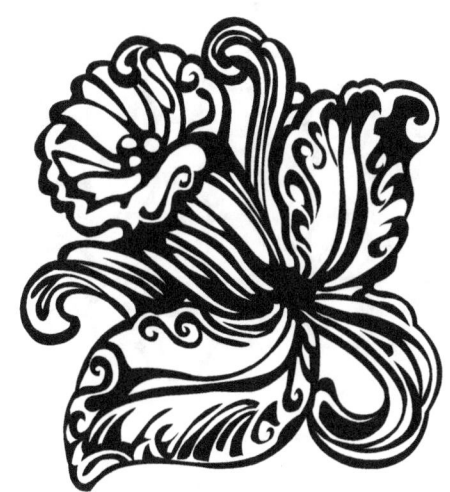

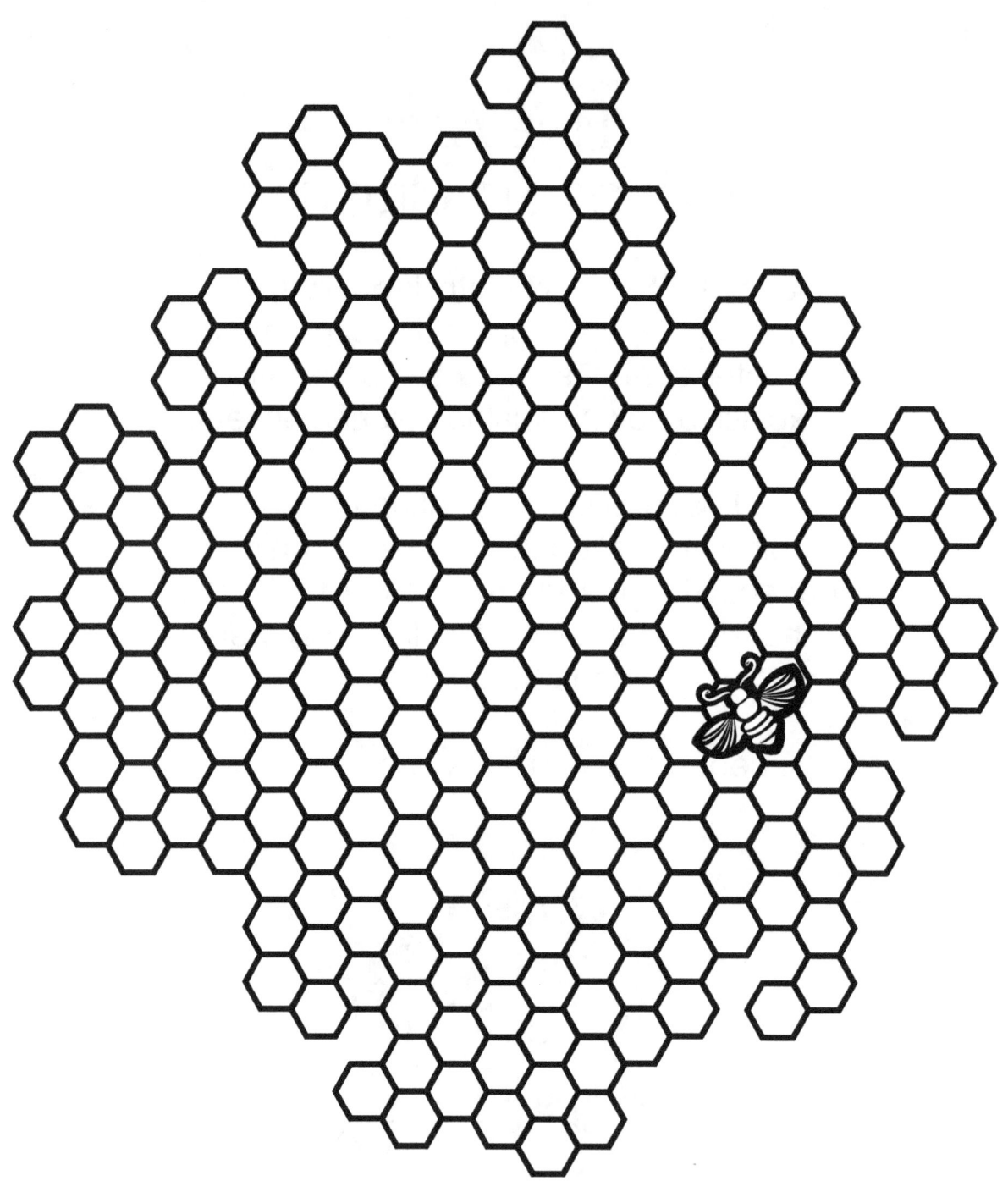

ART ESCAPES™

COLOR COMPOSITION TEST PAGE

FAQ About Copyright Law

Can I share an image I colored on Facebook?
Just include **fineartcoloring.com** in the post and go right ahead!
Consider joining the *Fine Art Coloring Group*
on Facebook so we all can see your work! :)

Can I copy uncolored pages to share?
This is illegal as it impacts the income of the artist.
And if images are shared online, search engine image searches
will find them as we keep up with our copyright maintenance.

How do I get legal, free sheets for a party or activity?
Join the *Fine Art Coloring Group* on Facebook
to download select PDF coloring sheets.
Not on Facebook? Just sign up to **fineartcoloring.com**.
It's free, easy, and your sheets will always look great.

What is a Derivative Copyright?
A vector illustration carefully crafted from the original work is
protected as many artistic decisions were made in the process.
Therefore, they are protected under the Derivative Copyright Law.
Colorists should learn more about this law as well.

Your work as a colorist is valuable!
Find out how to protect your work at **fineartcoloring.com**.
Sign up and introduce yourself. Every new colored page is
a collaboration between artists and I'd love to meet you!

Color on my friends!

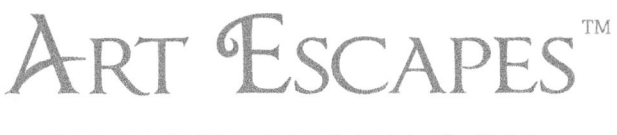

ART ESCAPES™

Fine Art Coloring Books

This book has been brought to you by
Kozlansky.com and produced in harmony
with our mission to provide entertaining and
educational art & nature themed media.

Kozlansky.com is especially useful
for parents of public, private, and
homeschooled students who feel as though
visual arts & natural science subjects could
use a little boost.

Sign into Kozlansky.com for more
information and access to full free content.

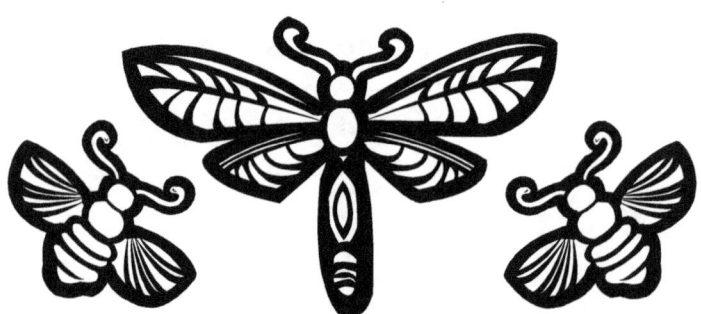

KOZLANSKY.COM

ENTERTAIN - EDUCATE - INSPIRE